SCIENTIFIC AMERICAN EXPLORES BIG IDEAS

The Size of the Universe

AF753903

The Editors of *Scientific American*

SCIENTIFIC AMERICAN | EDUCATIONAL PUBLISHING

New York

Published in 2027 by Scientific American Educational Publishing
in association with **The Rosen Publishing Group**
2544 Clinton Street, Buffalo NY 14224

Contains material from Scientific American®, a division of Springer Nature America, Inc., reprinted by permission, as well as original material from The Rosen Publishing Group®.

Copyright © 2027 Scientific American® and Rosen Publishing Group®.

All rights reserved.

First Edition

Scientific American
Lisa Pallatroni: Project Editor

Rosen Publishing
Nicole Horning: Compiling Editor
Michael Moy: Senior Graphic Designer

Cataloging-in-Publication Data
Names: Scientific American, Inc.
Title: The size of the universe / edited by the Scientific American Editors.
Description: Buffalo, New York : Scientific American Educational Publishing, an imprint of Rosen Publishing, 2027. | Series: Scientific American explores big ideas | Includes glossary and index.
Identifiers: ISBN 9781538314616 (pbk.) | ISBN 9781538314623 (library bound) | ISBN 9781538314630 (ebook)
Subjects: LCSH: Cosmology–Juvenile literature. | Expanding universe–Juvenile literature. | Black holes (Astronomy)–Juvenile literature. | Universe–Juvenile literature
Classification: LCC QB983.S594 2027 | DDC 523.1–dc23

Manufactured in the United States of America
Websites listed were live at the time of publication.

Cover: Triff/Shutterstock.com

CPSIA Compliance Information: Batch # CS27SA.
For Further Information contact Rosen Publishing at 1-800-237-9932.

Published in 2027 by Scientific American Educational Publishing
in association with **The Rosen Publishing Group**
2544 Clinton Street, Buffalo NY 14224

Contains material from Scientific American®, a division of Springer Nature America, Inc., reprinted by permission, as well as original material from The Rosen Publishing Group®.

Copyright © 2027 Scientific American® and Rosen Publishing Group®.

All rights reserved.

First Edition

Scientific American
Lisa Pallatroni: Project Editor

Rosen Publishing
Nicole Horning: Compiling Editor
Michael Moy: Senior Graphic Designer

Cataloging-in-Publication Data
Names: Scientific American, Inc.
Title: The size of the universe / edited by the Scientific American Editors.
Description: Buffalo, New York : Scientific American Educational Publishing, an imprint of Rosen Publishing, 2027. | Series: Scientific American explores big ideas | Includes glossary and index.
Identifiers: ISBN 9781538314616 (pbk.) | ISBN 9781538314623 (library bound) | ISBN 9781538314630 (ebook)
Subjects: LCSH: Cosmology–Juvenile literature. | Expanding universe–Juvenile literature. | Black holes (Astronomy)–Juvenile literature. | Universe–Juvenile literature
Classification: LCC QB983.S594 2027 | DDC 523.1–dc23

Manufactured in the United States of America
Websites listed were live at the time of publication.

Cover: Triff/Shutterstock.com

CPSIA Compliance Information: Batch # CS27SA.
For Further Information contact Rosen Publishing at 1-800-237-9932.

CONTENTS

INTRODUCTION

The size of the universe is nearly impossible to imagine. How big is it, really? Where does it end? Does it even have an end? What's going on in space, anyway? From here on Earth, the night sky can seem small, filled with tiny bits of light. But each of those points may be something massive, far away, and much more complex than it appears. The more scientists explore and learn about space, the more they realize how vast it is and how much we don't truly know about.

Understanding the size of the universe is about more than numbers. Distances in space are so large that familiar units like miles or kilometers no longer make sense, and even light, which is the fastest thing we know, takes years to make it from one point to another. As technology improves, scientists are able to observe farther into space, uncovering new objects and phenomena that challenge what we thought we knew. Each discovery helps us learn more about space, but it also reminds us how much is unknown.

In this book, you'll explore different parts of the universe and what they reveal about its size and structure. You'll start by learning about other planets, then you'll discover the strange and unexpected in Anomalies in Space. Then, you'll explore some of the most mysterious objects in the universe: black holes. The Stars takes a closer look at the massive, burning spheres that shape galaxies, followed by exploring the galaxies themselves in the chapter In a Galaxy Far, Far Away.

Trying to understand the size of the universe means thinking beyond your everyday experience. The scale is so large that it's difficult to picture, yet scientists find ways to study and explain it. With new tools and research, our understanding keeps growing, revealing an interesting atmosphere more complex that ever imagined.

Section 1: The Planets

Jupiter Isn't as Huge as We Thought It Was

By Jackie Flynn Mogensen

The solar system's most giant planet is slightly less of a giant than scientists once thought. Jupiter, a planet so huge it could hold 1,000 Earths, is 8 kilometers less wide at its equator and 24 kilometers flatter at its poles, according to a new study.

The new measurements overturn almost 50 years-worth of consensus about the size and shape of the planet.

"Textbooks will need to be updated," Yohai Kaspi, a professor at the Weizmann Institute of Science in Israel and the senior author on the study, said in a statement. "The size of Jupiter hasn't changed, of course, but the way we measure it has."

Previously, scientists relied on observations by the Voyager and Pioneer spacecraft, which were launched by NASA in the 1970s. But NASA's Juno mission, which launched in 2011 and which reached Jupiter in 2016, has proved a game-changer: By passing behind the planet for the first time, it allowed for clearer observations of Jupiter's size.

The research means scientists have to adjust their models of Jupiter, a change that will have resounding implications both for studies of the planet's features, like its volatile atmosphere, but also for understanding how gas giants like Jupiter formed in the first place.

"Jupiter was likely the first planet to form in the solar system," Kaspi said in the same statement, "and by studying what's happening inside it, we get closer to understanding how the solar system, and planets like ours, came to be."

About the Author

Jackie Flynn Mogensen is a breaking news reporter at Scientific American. *Before joining* SciAm, *she was a science reporter at* Mother Jones, *where she received a National Academies Eric and Wendy Schmidt Award for Excellence in Science Communications in 2024. Mogensen holds a master's degree in environmental communication and a bachelor's degree in earth sciences from Stanford University. She is based in New York City.*

Another Earth or a Blip in the Data? We May Never Find Out

By Joseph Howlett

Astronomers think they've found a celestial unicorn: a potentially habitable near twin of Earth with the same size and perhaps even year-length as our own familiar planet, circling a star much like our own. The only problem is that they're not sure it's really there.

The first—and so far only—hint of the potential planet arrived in observations from NASA's now retired Kepler space telescope. In 2017 the telescope recorded a sudden 10-hour-long dimming of HD 137010, a star only slightly less massive and luminous than our sun that is located some 146 light-years away in the constellation of Libra. Initially flagged by volunteers sifting through archival Kepler data as part of the crowdsourced Planet Hunters project, the signal matched the profile of a tiny, rocky exoplanet passing—or transiting—in front of the star. After further analysis, a team of astronomers reported the possible discovery on Tuesday in the *Astrophysical Journal Letters*.

If confirmed, this world would officially be called HD 137010 b—but confirmation has proved difficult, to say the least.

Kepler's search strategy was to stare at a rich field of stars for years on end. By watching for telltale transits, it discovered thousands of exoplanets. Stars can dim for many nonplanetary reasons, however. So the mission's scientists sought a total of three observed transits for Kepler's smallest planetary candidates before the researchers would declare them to be genuine worlds. This time-consuming process was cut short a few years into the mission when the telescope's stabilizing instruments failed, forcing NASA to switch Kepler's field of view to new patches of sky. This new phase of the mission was called K2, and each of its campaigns only lasted about 80 days. One of them brought the sole known transit of HD 137010 b.

By the time anyone noticed that single, tantalizing signal in Kepler's vast dataset, the telescope had been mothballed, decommissioned into a graveyard orbit after running out of fuel.

"The authors have tried to rule out everything they can from the data, but with only one transit, you can only do so much," says Jessie Christiansen, an astrophysicist at the California Institute of Technology.

"There's always something that could go wrong with a single transit," says Andrew Vanderburg, an astronomer at Harvard University, who co-authored the study. "That being said, it's a very strong signal–it looks like a planet."

Vanderburg and his colleagues did manage to roughly gauge the candidate's orbital speed–and with that, constrain its plausible orbital period and distance from its star. But even so, HD 137010 b could have a year lasting anywhere from about 300 to 550 days, the authors say. That huge range not only complicates the search for more transits; it also means this notional near twin of Earth could be so far from its slightly-dimmer star that it would instead be more like a frozen, supersized version of Mars.

Confirmation seems unlikely, for now. No other exoplanet-hunting telescope currently plans to even look at the star, let alone scrutinize it long enough to bag more transits. "Two transits is a maybe, but three transits is exactly what you want," Christiansen says. "It's a little soon to fire up the rockets and head for this star." But because the star is so relatively bright and nearby in the Milky Way, it could make a desirable target for future planned observatories that will be capable of finding small exoplanets by taking their pictures.

Yet even that might be a stretch. Why devote a multibillion-dollar space telescope to looking for a possible planet when other, more certain worlds could be studied instead? Vanderburg points out as well that even some exoplanets that had previously been thought to be confirmed via three transits have turned out to be likely mirages. This one seems different, though, because of the strength and clarity of its sadly solitary signal. "I feel better about that one transit than I feel about multiple transits from some of these other systems," he says.

Still, he wishes the astronomers planning Kepler's original mission could have magically foreseen what this otherwise unremarkable star may be hiding. "If we'd stared at it for four years," he says, "this would have been the 'Earth 2.0' that no one could dispute."

About the Author

Joseph Howlett is a staff reporter at Scientific American *covering physics, math, astronomy and more. He was previously a math staff writer at* Quanta Magazine, *and holds a Ph.D. in particle physics from Columbia University.*

Scientists Just Clocked a 'Rogue' Planet the Size of Saturn

By Jackie Flynn Mogensen

When we imagine a planet, we think of one like ours, orbiting a star. But some have a far lonelier existence, drifting through interstellar space without a sun to call their own. Known as "rogue" or "free-floating" planets, these worlds are often challenging to study. With no known star and no orbit from which to estimate their size, they've generally flown under the radar—until now.

In a new study published in *Science* on Thursday, scientists show how they measured the mass of one such rogue planet for the first time—a breakthrough that could enable further studies of these strange lonely worlds.

Instead of looking at the planet's orbit, the research team, led by Subo Dong of Peking University, instead analyzed how the planet's gravity bent the light from a distant star, in a so-called microlensing event, from two separate vantage points: Earth and the now-retired Gaia space observatory.

The technique resembles how our eyes' depth perception works, Dong says: the microlensing event was seen by Gaia about two hours later than by scientists on Earth. That difference in time allowed the researchers to measure the planet's distance and estimate its mass.

"What's really great about this work, and really noteworthy, is that it's the first time we've got a mass for these objects," says Gavin Coleman, a postdoctoral researcher at Queen Mary University of London, who authored a related commentary also published in *Science* but was not involved in the study. "This was purely because the authors had both ground-based observations and Gaia, looking at observations from two different places."

What they found is that the planet has about the same mass as Saturn. But the findings also offer a hint about its past: "Knowing [its mass] is the starting point," Dong says. "We can start to understand, okay, what could be the origin, the history of this planet?"

Dong hopes the study offers a jumping-off point for more research to better understand these mysterious cosmic bodies. That pursuit gets a boost later this year from NASA's Nancy Grace Roman Space Telescope, set to launch in September, says David Bennet, a senior research scientist at the University of Maryland, College Park, and NASA. Able to image the entire sky 1,000 times faster than the Hubble Space Telescope can, Roman could help identify hundreds of rogue planets. And with this work, researchers will have a way to estimate their masses, too.

"The door is open to study this new emerging population of planets," Dong says.

About the Author

Jackie Flynn Mogensen is a breaking news reporter at Scientific American. *Before joining* SciAm, *she was a science reporter at* Mother Jones, *where she received a National Academies Eric and Wendy Schmidt Award for Excellence in Science Communications in 2024. Mogensen holds a master's degree in environmental communication and a bachelor's degree in earth sciences from Stanford University. She is based in New York City.*

How Far are We from Finding Exomoons and Exorings?

By Phil Plait

If you examine our solar system's giant planets, you'll notice right away that they've all got moons—a *lot* of moons. While Earth only has the one, Jupiter has about 100 that we know of (and likely hundreds more, depending on what you define as a "moon," that is). Saturn has almost 275!

Many of these moons are huge; Saturn's Titan and Jupiter's Ganymede are both about the size of Mercury, and if they orbited the sun on their own, we'd be sorely tempted to call them planets in their own right.

As if moons weren't enough, our quartet of beefier planets (including Uranus and Neptune) also sport rings. Saturn's, of course, are the most obvious and iconic, but the others have rings as well, albeit ones that are fainter and harder to see.

So moons and rings alike seem to be easy for giant planets to make—at least around the sun. Presumably this holds true for the myriad large worlds we've discovered orbiting other stars; many of these exoplanets should have exomoons and exorings, too.

But could we detect them?

The answer, so common with astronomy, is *maybe*.

Astronomers have found several exomoon candidates already. We can't see them directly—they're too faint and too close to their parent planets to resolve—but their presence can be inferred.

One of the most noteworthy exomoon candidates, Kepler-1625b I, was first identified in 2017. The year before, astronomers had discovered its exoplanet via the transit method: we happen to see the planet's orbit edge on, so once per orbit, we can see the planet passing—transiting—directly in front of its star, creating a mini eclipse. These transits usually manifest as a U- or V-shaped dip in the star's brightness when plotted over time. Such a plot is called a light curve.

With the exoplanet Kepler-1625b, there were some asymmetries, however—odd bumps in its associated light curve that were difficult to explain. Astronomers posited that this could be caused by an orbiting exomoon that sometimes trails and sometimes leads the planet itself during their mutual transit, changing the light curve's shape. If it's real, this exomoon would have to be quite large; its telltale bump in the light curve would correspond to something about the size of Neptune. (The exoplanet itself is a so-called super-Jupiter, a gargantuan world that could have the equivalent mass of a dozen Jupiters.) This claimed exomoon has proved controversial, however, with papers going back and forth arguing for or against its existence. For the moment, it's still a candidate, unconfirmed.

Another exomoon-hunting method relies on transit timing variations. As the exomoon orbits its host, its gravity swings the planet around their common center of gravity, called the barycenter. This subtly changes the timing of the planet's transits, altering their predicted onset or duration by small amounts. Certain configurations—such as a very large moon orbiting a relatively low-mass planet—should produce timing variations that could be detected in existing data, although nontransiting planets can induce similar signals, complicating the exomoon search.

Astrometry is another promising technique; this is the very precise measurement of an astronomical object's position and movement in the sky. It can potentially reveal an unseen exomoon by its offset to its host's barycenter, which manifests as a wobble in the planet's motion around the star. Some interferometers, such as the GRAVITY instrument on the Very Large Telescope in Chile, can measure positions with such astonishing accuracy that detecting the wobbles of hidden exomoons might be possible for some giant exoplanets around nearby stars.

In January a team of astronomers reported how they used GRAVITY's astrometric measurements to study HD 206893, a star with a companion called HD 206893 B, which is likely a brown dwarf with a mass about 20 times that of Jupiter. While it's not technically an exoplanet, this brown dwarf could still harbor a detectable exomoon. And indeed, the team found some borderline evidence for a companion. If their observed astrometric wobble motion is real, it implies that HD 206893 B is accompanied by something in a nine-month orbit with an estimated mass *nearly half that of Jupiter*.

This "moon" would be more than 100 times Earth's mass—hence the quotation marks—and, like all other exomoon candidates, remains as yet unconfirmed. Astronomers are, however, currently testing a sharper-eyed upgrade to GRAVITY (aptly called GRAVITY+) that should be able to eventually validate or rule out this particular candidate.

Yet another exomoon search method involves looking for them via—of all things—volcanic activity. This isn't as farfetched as it sounds; Jupiter's moon Io erupts constantly, blasting sulfur into space as its innards are heated by gravitational tides raised by the giant planet and other nearby moons. In recent years astronomers have used the James Webb Space Telescope (JWST) and other observatories to look at the exoplanet WASP-39b, and they've detected a cloud in its vicinity that contains fluctuating amounts of sulfur dioxide and other compounds. The fluctuations hint at an episodic, external source—potentially eruptions from a sort of super-Io satellite being tidally squeezed by its hefty planetary host. This detection—and another much like it, around a different exoplanet, WASP-49Ab—isn't conclusive, but it shows promise as a new pathway for finding these elusive exomoons.

And what of exorings? In some ways, they may be harder to detect than exomoons. Rings, while wide and bright, can actually be fairly ethereal; all the material in Saturn's rings only add up to a sphere about 400 kilometers across, about the size of its midsize moons. The gravitational effects from such puny accoutrements would be too small for astronomers to see.

But exorings around a transiting exoplanet may sometimes block enough starlight to register as a series of shallow dips in a star's light curve. Something like this has already been seen; the star 1SWASP J140747.93-394542.6 (or J1407 for short) exhibited a series of extreme dimming events in 2007. One possible explanation is that the dimming was the shadowy transit of a planet, J1407b, surrounded by a huge disk of material. If so, the ring system is immense, possibly 180 million km across, bigger than the distance of Earth from the sun. Neither the planet nor its rings have been confirmed in follow-up observations, however, leading astronomers to pursue other possible explanations.

There may be another way to spot exorings. In the November 2025 edition of the *Astronomical Journal*, a team of astronomers posited using JWST to look for them. While any rings would be far too small to see directly, the scientists note that icy rings will reflect infrared light strongly at certain shorter wavelengths but not nearly so well at longer ones. If an exoplanet seen by JWST exhibits this pattern, it may be because of the presence of exorings.

The team found that an exoring system would have to be fairly large for this to work because JWST couldn't detect this effect for any ring system smaller than about three times the extent of Saturn's. One that was 10 times the size of Saturn's, however, could be within JWST's reach, provided its exoplanet host wasn't too close to its far brighter star. The scientists also note in their paper that NASA's proposed Habitable Worlds Observatory and the space agency's soon-to-launch Nancy Grace Roman Space Telescope might also be able to detect exorings this way as well.

We may have far to go before we find either exomoons or exorings with certainty. But looking at our own giant planets, I suspect those discoveries are a matter of when, not if.

About the Author

Phil Plait is a professional astronomer and science communicator in Virginia. His column for Scientific American, *The Universe, covers all things space. He writes the* Bad Astronomy Newsletter. *Follow him online.*

Section 2: Anomalies in Space

The Universe Is Static. No, Expanding! Wait, Slowing? Oh, Accelerating

By Richard Panek

To astronomers in the 1990s, these three facts were self-evident: The universe is expanding; all the matter in the universe is gravitationally attracting all the other matter in the universe; therefore, the expansion of the universe is slowing.

Two scientific collaborations assigned themselves the task of determining the rate of that deceleration. Find that rate, they figured, and they would know nothing less than the fate of the universe. Is the expansion slowing just enough that it will eventually come to a halt? Or is it slowing so much that it will eventually stop, reverse itself and result in a kind of big bang boomerang?

The answer, which the two teams reached independently in 1998, was precisely the opposite of what they expected.

The expansion of the universe isn't slowing down. It's speeding up.

Cosmology has often lent itself to unthinking assumptions that turned out to be exactly wrong. The ur-example is geocentrism. Over the couple of millennia before the invention of the telescope in the early 1600s, the occasional philosopher suggested Earth orbits the sun and not the other way around. But the vast majority of astronomers could simply look up and see for themselves. The sun orbits Earth. The evidence was, well, self-evident.

But then, most of the history of astronomy had relied on an unthinking assumption: The heavens would always be out of reach. Like the prisoners in Plato's parable, we would forever be at the mercy of our perceptual limitations, trying to make sense of the motions in a two-dimensional celestial realm that was the cosmic equivalent of a cave wall. The invention of the telescope in the first decade of the 17th century overturned both those assumptions: Earth orbits the sun; the heavens are at our fingertips.

More telescopic discoveries followed that, to varying extents, contradicted one self-evident "fact" after another: mountains on the moon, moons around Jupiter, new stars, new planets. Some assumptions turned out to have been not just unthinking but unthinkable. How could anyone in the history of civilization ever have looked at Saturn and thought, "I'm assuming it doesn't have rings"?

That the universe is expanding–the major premise leading to the 1990s search for the deceleration rate–was a revelation that nobody saw coming, including the two theorists who made the discovery not only conceivable but inevitable.

The first, Isaac Newton, would have had to make two counterintuitive leaps of logic to reach such a shocking conclusion. He would have needed to imagine that the universe was capable of doing what it self-evidently was not doing: collapsing. Then he would have needed to conceive of it as doing the opposite: getting bigger.

Albert Einstein, the second theorist who paved the way for the expansion discovery, did conceive of it. In November 1915 he presented the equations underlying his general theory of relativity; 15 months later he applied those equations to, as he phrased the topic in the paper's title, "cosmological considerations." According to his math, the universe should be volatile over time, either expanding or contracting. To avoid that unsettling implication, he introduced a variable, L, the Greek symbol for lambda, to balance his equation. The value of lambda would be whatever it needed to be to satisfy Einstein's preference for a universe in perfect balance.

Each theorist's "blunder," as Einstein characterized his own refusal to trust his math, was understandable. Newton and Einstein, however intellectually exceptional, were still only human. The universe was static. If evidence to the contrary existed, it certainly wasn't obvious.

And then it was. In the early 1920s American astronomer Edwin Hubble deployed the new 100-inch telescope atop Mount Wilson in California to observe some of the nebulous smudges at the farthest reaches of previous telescopes. Using Cepheid variables (stars that brighten and dim with clockwork regularity) as a measure of distance, he inferred that at least some of those nebulae were actually "island universes"–galaxies–beyond our own Milky Way. Next he used the redshifts of those galaxies to infer not only that the galaxies are moving away from us and from one another–itself a science-redefining discovery–but also their rate.

When Hubble plotted those distances against those velocities on an x/y graph, he found a direct correlation: the more distant the galaxies, the faster they were moving away from us. Thus, the universe must be expanding. Belgian astronomer Georges Lemaître independently reached the same conclusion, working not from his own data but from Einstein's equations. Trace the expansion backward, he argued, and you would arrive at a "primeval atom."

Evidence supporting the existence of such a "big bang" didn't come until 1964, in the form of a background of microwave radiation that seems to pervade all of space. Theorists had predicted the existence of such a background as the relic of an explosive origin, although the two Bell Labs astronomers who first detected the radiation initially dismissed it as noise, possibly the result of pigeon droppings lining the giant horn of their radio antenna. Four physicists at nearby Princeton University, however, recognized that the observation matched the key prediction of the big bang theory.

Six years later American astronomer Allan Sandage cast cosmology as "the search for two numbers." One number was the "rate of expansion" now. The other, however, harbored the unthinking assumption that would motivate two teams of researchers a quarter of a century later: "the deceleration in the expansion" over time.

Both teams trying to measure cosmic deceleration followed Hubble's methodology of plotting velocity versus distance on a graph (using the magnitudes of a type of exploding star, or supernova, rather than Cepheid variables). Both collaborations expected to find the same direct correlation that Hubble did–at least at first. At some distance, though, they assumed that the line would depart from its 45-degree trajectory and dip, indicating that the apparent magnitudes of the supernovae were brighter, and therefore nearer, than they would be in a universe expanding at a constant rate.

And depart from its 45-degree trajectory the line did. Only it didn't dip. It rose. The supernovae were dimmer, and thus farther away, than they would be in a universe expanding at a constant rate. The expansion of the universe, the rival teams concluded, isn't slowing down. It's somehow speeding up.

Dark energy—as cosmologists came to call whatever was causing the acceleration—soon became part of the standard cosmological model, along with dark matter and "regular" matter, the stuff of us. Observations of the same cosmic microwave background that, back in the 1960s, helped to validate the big bang interpretation of cosmology have revealed the universe's ingredients. By studying the patterns in the radiation, scientists have refined the contributions to the mass-energy density of the universe to an exquisite level of precision: 4.9 percent of it must be ordinary matter, 26.8 percent dark matter, 68.3 percent dark energy. The model, cosmologists believe, is solid.

But not flawless. Not even complete. What is dark energy? What is dark matter? Indeed, even after all these years: What is the fate of the universe? Just this year the Dark Energy Spectroscopic Instrument in Arizona provided evidence that dark energy may have changed over the course of the evolution of the universe. Cosmologists have found the evidence compelling, though its meaning—let alone its implications for the standard model of cosmology—remains elusive.

So: Is cosmology on the precipice of another reversal? Another revolution? If history is any guide, the answer is: Maybe. For all today's cosmologists know, they might be laboring under a seemingly unassailable, self-evident, yet incorrect assumption. Perhaps even an unthinking one.

It's happened before.

About the Author

Richard Panek is the prizewinning author of Pillars of Creation *(Little, Brown, 2024).*

The James Webb Space Telescope Could Solve One of Cosmology's Deepest Mysteries

By Daniel Leonard

On Christmas morning of 2021, astronomers watched their new, greatest tool successfully blast off into space. Now the James Webb Space Telescope (JWST) is fully deployed and has arrived at its deep-space destination, a quiet locale 1.5 million kilometers beyond Earth.

Massimo Stiavelli heads the JWST Mission Office at the institute that allocates research time on the telescope. According to Stiavelli, "every area of science is covered" in the proposals his group has approved, from the search for potentially habitable exoplanets to studies of the earliest stars. Yet he is particularly hopeful that JWST could help settle one of the biggest controversies in modern astronomy: the dispute about the expansion rate of the universe.

"If you try to measure the current expansion rate, well, there's a variety of techniques that people use, and they tend to get a certain number," says Tommaso Treu, an astrophysicist at the University of California, Los Angeles. "And it turns out that those numbers don't match."

Measurements of the universe's expansion rate, known as the Hubble constant, currently cluster around two figures: 67 and 73. Each number is an expression of the same thing—the kilometers-per-second rate of cosmic expansion per every megaparsec (roughly 3.26 million light-years) of space. Although seemingly slight, the difference between these figures is enormous in comparison with the high-precision agreement that exists for other cosmological measurements. Simply put, something is not adding up.

Researchers are not sure how to account for this discrepancy, which they call the Hubble tension. It may just be an error resulting from the different ways the Hubble constant is being measured. Otherwise, the tension could spell trouble for our current understanding of physics, forcing theorists to revisit (and perhaps even discard) some of their most cherished models.

"The quest to measure the expansion rate goes back around 100 years," says Adam Riess, an astrophysicist at Johns Hopkins University. Scientists taking part in that quest fall into two main camps.

The first camp gathers data from the very early universe. These researchers rely on the cosmic microwave background, a residual glow of radiation from roughly 400,000 years after the big bang. By taking measurements from the cosmic microwave background and extrapolating them into the present using our best physical models, astronomers in this camp can reach an estimate for the expansion rate of the universe today. Their calculations indicate that the Hubble constant is around 67.

But Riess adds that JWST will not improve measurements of this kind. Microwaves from the early universe have wavelengths that are too long for JWST—which focuses on infrared light—to detect. Instead JWST has the potential to improve results from the other camp (of which Riess is a prominent member): local measurements.

"Local" is a relative term. Here, it refers to measurements of the Hubble constant that hinge on calculating the distances to stars and galaxies, which may be "only" millions of light-years away. "Measuring distances is what you need to measure the Hubble constant because the Hubble constant is how distances change over time," Treu says.

Astronomers have found a few ways to gauge such celestial distances. Most of them rely on "standard candles," astronomical objects of known brightness. By comparing such an object's actual, intrinsic brightness with its apparent brightness through a telescope, observers can reliably determine its distance from Earth.

Wendy Freedman, an astronomer at the University of Chicago, uses a certain class of red giant stars as her preferred standard candle. "The physics [of these stars] leads to this standard luminosity," which makes them perfect distance indicators, Freedman explains.

Using the Hubble Space Telescope to observe these red giants, Freedman's team arrived at an estimate for the Hubble constant in 2019: roughly 70.

That is on the low end of local estimates. (In fact, it is vexingly midway between the standard values embraced by each camp.) According to Riess, whose standard-candle work uses supernovae and Cepheid variable stars instead of red giants, most local studies have produced somewhat higher values for the Hubble constant–some as high as 75, with an average around 73.

This is a much bigger range than the measurements out of the early-universe camp. Likewise, local studies tend to have greater "error bars" (or uncertainties) than studies that use early-universe data.

That is where JWST can help. By observing in the infrared spectrum, it will be able to look straight through pesky clouds of space dust that all too often interfere with local astronomers' measurements. The Hubble Space Telescope–the previous tool of choice for local astronomers–has far more modest infrared capabilities; its infrared measurements come at the expense of lower image quality. As Riess explains, JWST can do both: observe in infrared and maintain high-resolution imaging.

Crisper, dust-free images: that's the JWST promise.

JWST is such a technological improvement that, rather than altering their methods, many astronomers are planning to carefully replicate their prior research in order to see if the results change. Both Riess and Freedman have been granted research time on JWST to do just that.

Whether or not their results *will* change is uncertain. It is possible that data from JWST could lead local studies to cluster around an estimate for the Hubble constant as low as the one from the early-universe camp. But that seems very unlikely: Riess points out that virtually no local study has produced a result so low, just as no early-universe study has produced a result as high as 73.

So what would it mean if local studies again cluster around 73 but this time with even greater precision? According to Treu, that would imply the Hubble tension is a real discrepancy and not just the result of study error.

If so, Treu adds, that would probably point to something fundamentally absent in our understanding of physics. Because early universe studies rely on physical models to extrapolate their primordial data into the present, missing physics could be the reason those studies are producing a figure as low as 67.

What sort of missing physics? "It could be another neutrino," Riess says. "It could be an early episode of dark energy. It could be decaying dark matter. It could be primordial magnetic fields. All of these have been suggested as things that would help mitigate or explain this." But Riess points out that none of these have "a strong second line of evidence" besides the fact that they could help explain the Hubble tension.

Likewise, Freedman notes that most of these ideas wind up "wrecking" other, agreed on parts of physics somewhere along the line. "This turns out to be really difficult to solve–which is not to say somebody's not going to come up with a brilliant idea at some point," Freedman says.

There may be a hole in physics. There is no guarantee that JWST will help us figure out how to fill it. But by giving greater insight into the Hubble tension, JWST can at least help confirm that the hole is really there.

About the Author

Daniel Leonard is a freelance science journalist and former Scientific American *editorial intern whose work focuses on space, tech and natural history. Follow Leonard on Twitter @dalorleon*

Physicists Propose a Simpler, Hotter Origin for the Cosmos

By Stephanie Pappas

For a fraction of a second after the big bang occurred 13.8 billion years ago, most physicists believe, the newborn universe dramatically ballooned in size, jumping from being smaller than a proton to being bigger than a softball. Such an exponential expansion may seem minor, but it is equivalent to a grape in the palm of your hand swelling to become tens of thousands of times larger than the observable universe. Known as cosmic inflation, this strange, fleeting period is usually considered to have been an expansion of near nothingness because, at the time, most of the universe's elementary particles had yet to blink into existence. In other words, the standard view of cosmic inflation suggests the universe didn't really begin as a hot, dense fireball but rather as a cold void that only later reheated into a plasmatic soup of particles by some poorly understood process.

But a new theoretical study published in the journal *Physical Review Letters* suggests that inflation may have been warm from the start. In fact, the researchers find, a warm period of inflation that began to populate the universe with matter could have naturally arisen from interactions within physics' Standard Model, the theory that describes the fundamental forces and elementary particles in the universe.

"What we have shown with this paper is that actually being warm during inflation is extremely generic and extremely simple," says its lead author Kim Berghaus, a postdoctoral scholar in theoretical physics at the California Institute of Technology. The solution to the problem of cold inflation requires only one unconfirmed type of particle, she says. "It takes us to this footing of 'This may have actually occurred in nature, and we can go look for it,'" Berghaus adds.

Inflation itself is a big mystery. Most physicists think it happened in the first 0.000000000000000000000000000000001 second (10^{-32} second) of cosmic time, by which point the universe had expanded by a factor of as much as 10^{50}. The reason anyone takes this mind-boggling idea seriously is that it would explain what the big bang alone can't–namely, why the universe appears so extremely uniform at very large scales. Studies of the big bang's afterglow–an all-sky whisper of radiation called the cosmic microwave background, or CMB–show it to be basically the same everywhere. The most straightforward way to account for this preternatural smoothness is a period of inflation that provides time for the baby universe to reach a uniform temperature.

Meanwhile inflation would also have magnified tiny random fluctuations in the early universe, creating density variations in the primordial plasma. These acted as seeds for cosmic structures; as their gravity glommed together more matter, denser regions would eventually grow to become star-filled galaxies and galaxy clusters.

As of yet, there is no direct observational evidence for inflation, so sorting out its details is a task for theorists. Initially, physicists envisioned inflation as a cold process that involved energy fields that permeated all of space. It was powered by a field with high potential energy, called the inflaton field, which behaved a bit like a ball rolling down a hill and transforming its potential energy into kinetic energy as it descends. In the beginning, this "hill" was gentle, almost flat, and as the inflaton "ball" rolled down, the exponentially expanding universe rapidly became less dense. The "hill" eventually bottomed out when the expanding universe was diluted to nearly a vacuum. At this point, the rolling inflaton "ball" could essentially carom around the resulting "valley," unleashing its kinetic energy to create many elementary particles and reheat the universe. Only then did the "newborn universe as fireball" scenario proceed.

But precisely how this reheating step would have occurred wasn't well-understood, says Vahid Kamali, a visiting professor at McGill University and an associate professor at Bu-Ali Sina University in Iran, who studies early-universe cosmology and wasn't involved in the new research. Physicists wondered if this step was needed or if there was a way for the whole inflationary process to stay warm.

Arjun Berera, a theoretical physicist at the University of Edinburgh, who was also not involved in the new study, was the first to propose warm inflation in 1995. Cold inflation was in some ways too simple, Berera says. "When systems interact, we expect there to be friction and particle production," he says. "And inflation, in the standard picture, didn't have that."

Berera's first model was initially dismissed. Critics argued that warm inflation would have effectively burned itself out, prematurely churning out interacting particles that would have sapped its potential energy. In the hill analogy, the inflaton "ball" would have suddenly plunged down a too-steep slope, bringing the whole process to an abrupt end.

"The challenge has always been how to find the model that produces the particles but doesn't make such a steep hill," Berera says.

Berera and his colleagues published a paper in 2016 that found such a model using interactions and fields similar to those known in the Standard Model. Berghaus and her co-authors Marco Drewes of the University of Louvain in Belgium and Sebastian Zell of Ludwig Maximilian University of Munich take this a step further in their new paper, firmly situating warm inflation in the Standard Model itself. Their calculations show that a feeble interaction between the inflaton field and elementary particles called gluons would be sufficient to warm up inflation. Gluons carry the strong nuclear force, which glues together fundamental particles called quarks to make protons and neutrons.

"What they have done is to make this connection that you can have warm inflation with Standard Model interactions," says

Rudnei Ramos, a theoretical physicist at Rio de Janeiro State University in Brazil, who co-authored the 2016 paper but was not involved in the new study.

These Standard Model interactions would have heated the inflating universe, sidestepping the complication of needing a subsequent reheating phase. In cold inflation, the initial fluctuations are all quantum, Berera says, and must later transition to larger, so-called classical interactions during the reheating. The trouble is that no one really understands how that process unfolds. But in warm inflation, "it's not a big issue," he says, "because they're already classical."

The new model has one key caveat: the particle that creates the inflaton field is not yet known to exist. It would be a very light, chargeless particle called an axion, Berghaus says. Physicists have been on the quest for axions for decades because some possible variants of these particles might constitute most or all of the universe's dark matter. There are hints that axions might exist, including a faint background glow in space that was detected by the New Horizons spacecraft in 2022. If they do exist, trillions of them should be afloat in every cubic centimeter of the solar system. Projects such as the Axion Dark Matter Experiment, a collaboration of the University of Washington, Lawrence Livermore National Laboratory and other institutions, are currently hunting these particles by using intense magnetic fields to convert them to detectable microwave photons.

The new model's reliance on axions suggests that there are two avenues for eventual experimental validation—one via future surveys of the CMB to test some of the model's predictions and the other via ongoing laboratory-based searches for these elusive particles.

While the prospect of testability makes this new model very exciting, Kamali says, there is still much more to be done to reconcile it with other theories in cosmology. One example, he says, is that the size of the inflaton field in the new model doesn't match predictions from string theory. Even so, the allure of thoroughly explaining cosmic inflation within the Standard Model's well-known tenets is likely to prove irresistible for eager theorists and experimentalists alike.

"In our work, there is an opportunity for a discovery that can probe the connection between particle physics and the big bang," Berghaus says. "Because our proposed theory connects intimately with the Standard Model, it is testable."

About the Author

Stephanie Pappas is a freelance science journalist based in Denver, Colo.

AI Reveals 800 Never-Before-Seen "Cosmic Anomalies" in Old Hubble Images

By Jackie Flynn Mogensen

The universe is so vast, and the difficulty of discovering all that there is out in the cosmos is so great, that one might as well count all the grains of sand in the Sahara. But now, with the help of artificial intelligence, astronomers have revealed more than 800 previously unknown "cosmic anomalies" hidden in archival data from the Hubble Space Telescope.

Researchers at the European Space Agency (ESA) developed an AI tool that sifted through nearly 100 million image cutouts in the Hubble Legacy Archive, a collection of data from as early as 35 years ago. Incredibly, the AI took just two and a half days to run through the entire archive, a task that would have taken a human research team exponentially longer to accomplish.

The hunt turned up more than 1,300 "anomalous objects," including galaxy mergers, jellyfish galaxies (so named for their trailing tentacles of gas) and other unusual features. Among these were scores of possible gravitational lenses—spots where a massive object, such as a galaxy, bends the light of a given source, such as another galaxy—as well as dozens of other oddball objects that defied easy explanation. Of all the found objects, some 800 had never been described before.

The work was published last month in the journal *Astronomy & Astrophysics*.

In a statement, ESA data scientist and co-author on the paper Pablo Gómez said the AI approach could offer a model for exploring other space science archives. "It [shows] how useful this tool will be for other large datasets," he said.

About the Author

Jackie Flynn Mogensen is a breaking news reporter at Scientific American. *Before joining* SciAm, *she was a science reporter at* Mother Jones, *where she received a National Academies Eric and Wendy Schmidt Award for Excellence in Science Communications in 2024. Mogensen holds a master's degree in environmental communication and a bachelor's degree in earth sciences from Stanford University. She is based in New York City.*

Astronomers Are Agog over This All-Day Gamma-Ray Burst

By Yvette Cendes

You might think astronomers have seen it all, but the universe still throws us occasional new mysteries to keep us on our toes.

On July 2, 2025, observers around the world were alerted to a new gamma-ray burst (GRB), GRB 250702B, detected by NASA's Fermi Gamma-Ray Space Telescope. GRBs are extremely energetic explosions that rank among the most powerful astrophysical events in the universe, so luminous they can be seen from billions of light-years away. They're most commonly caused by either a merging pair of neutron stars or a very massive star ending its life in a supernova called a collapsar; in both of these "classical" cases, the resulting stellar cataclysm can spit out a giant, tightly focused jet of radiation and particles. When one of these jets is pointed directly at our solar system, we see it as a GRB.

They aren't *that* unusual to spot—the universe is so big and GRBs are so bright that astronomers see one or two a day on average. Even so, we soon realized something *very* unusual was happening with GRB 250702B. In the roughly half century of GRB studies, no one has ever seen one of these epic events last more than a few hours at most. Yet almost a full day elapsed before GRB 250702B faded away.

"The most surprising thing about this event is the duration of the emission. If it came from a GRB, it's the longest one ever detected," explains Adelle Goodwin, an astronomer at Curtin University in Australia, who is leading follow-up radio observations with the Very Large Array in New Mexico. Another oddity was that this GRB seemed to repeat, with astronomers seeing what appeared to be three distinct pulses across its nearly day-long duration; repetition would be strange because GRBs are normally so catastrophic that they effectively destroy their astrophysical sources, preventing any recurrence. Confronted with an enigma, scientists around the world scrambled to point every telescope they could at GRB 250702B to gather more clues.

Astronomers are not ones to shy away from a challenge, but GRB 250702B has provided us with several. First, its on-sky location fell within the star-and-dust-packed galactic plane of the Milky Way, making its true cosmic origins unclear; odds were that it occurred in some distant part of the universe, with its source obscured by dust, but in principle, whatever created the burst could have been inside our galaxy. Luckily, the James Webb Space Telescope was designed to peer through all that dust, allowing a team of researchers to reveal the truth in a recent preprint. GRB 250702B's still-mysterious origins trace back to a galaxy more than five billion light-years away from us. What's more, the galaxy itself is unusual: it's extremely large and dusty compared to most other galaxies and in fact is the biggest and brightest GRB-hosting galaxy anyone has ever seen. Astronomers can't yet say with certainty, but an unusual GRB coming from an unusual galaxy might be a clue in itself on what actually caused the explosion.

Of course, this is the real question behind GRB 250702B: What caused it? Theorists presently offer two main possibilities. This very odd GRB could have arisen from a particularly unusual collapse of a massive star that launched an abnormally energetic jet, or instead it could have come from a tidal disruption event (TDE) in which a white dwarf star was ripped apart and devoured by an intermediate-mass black hole weighing on the order of 100,000 solar masses. "The duration of GRB emission cannot be explained by classical collapsar scenarios, which means more exotic scenarios need to be invoked," Goodwin explains.

I recently attended this year's meeting of the American Astronomical Society's High-Energy Astrophysics Division (HEAD), presenting some of my own research on TDEs; suffice to say that speculation on GRB 250702B's origin dominated much of the informal sessions. "It's too long to be a GRB but not luminous enough to be a TDE at that distance," one of my colleagues confidently argued. Others were more cautious, pointing out that extraordinary claims require extraordinary evidence, and said they felt that threshold was not yet met for GRB 250702B. One thing is for sure: nothing quite drives excitement in a crowd of astronomers like an unusual signal none of us has seen before. (Despite all that excitement, many astronomers unfortunately declined to comment on the record for this story, citing a forthcoming NASA press release on GRB 250702B that is stuck in limbo because of the ongoing U.S. federal government shutdown.)

There are, of course, even wilder possibilities–it may be that this event represents some fantastic and heretofore entirely unwitnessed phenomenon. For example, a recent preprint argued that GRB 250702B actually arose from a black hole that merged with a star. This event would be exceedingly rare but should happen on some occasions, such as if two stars are orbiting in a pair and a larger one explodes, leaving behind a black hole. Over time, the gravitational interactions would cause the remaining star and its black hole companion to spiral together, culminating with a spectacular merger that would unleash unprecedented astrophysical fireworks.

Whatever its origin, GRB 250702B is exceptional, and it could be the first direct evidence of an entirely new kind of gigantic space explosion. Astronomers are still busy unraveling the full picture of where this space oddity fits in our strange and exciting universe.

About the Author

Yvette Cendes is a professor in the department of physics and astronomy at the University of Oregon. Follow her on Bluesky @whereisyvette.bsky.social

Section 3: Black Holes

How Big Can a Black Hole Be?

By Phil Plait

In the early 1960s astronomers discovered a monster.

Something in the constellation of Virgo was pouring out radio waves, but no counterpart in visible light was seen initially. After a lengthy effort, that changed when observers glimpsed a faint blue "star" sitting at the radio source's exact position. Eventually they were able to determine that this object, called 3C 273, was not a star at all but rather something much stranger located a staggering two billion light-years from Earth.

To be visible across such a vast stretch of space, the "quasi-stellar object" (quasar for short) 3C 273 had to be overwhelmingly bright. Scientists ultimately settled on a feeding black hole at the heart of a far-distant galaxy as the most likely engine for 3C 273's ridiculous luminosity. And it wasn't just any black hole but a positively Brobdingnagian one, with a mass that was probably 900 million times that of our sun.

Since that time, we've found many more such supermassive black holes. In fact, by the 1980s astronomers were starting to suspect that every big galaxy had a supermassive black hole in its center. Thanks to observations from the Hubble Space Telescope and other facilities, we now know that is true—which means there could be as many as a trillion such giants in the observable universe.

And "supermassive" is definitely the right name for them. Many have been found with a billion times the sun's mass, and the beefiest can be even heavier than that. This fact naturally raises the question: Just how hefty can one get?

Answering it, however, gets a bit tricky. A notional upper limit could pop out of mass measurements for many black holes, but such observations are difficult and often rely on indirect evidence and incomplete accounting of all the physics involved. With that in mind, though, this approach suggests that the biggest black holes top out around a few tens of billions of solar masses—that's as hefty as a smallish galaxy! Only a handful of these ultraheavyweights are known, and the uncertainties in their masses can be quite large.

If you could somehow offer up the entire universe as a meal, a black hole would happily consume it.

Still, is it possible that some could be even bigger? After all, in principle, a black hole could grow without end because these objects gain mass by eating anything and everything that gets too close; if you could somehow offer up the entire universe as a meal, a black hole would happily consume it.

But piling the entire cosmos on a black hole's dinner plate isn't very realistic, of course. According to research published in 2015 in the *Monthly Notices of the Royal Astronomical Society: Letters*, under physically possible (but implausibly ideal) conditions, the theoretical upper limit for a feeding, growing black hole should be a whopping 270 billion solar masses. More likely, though, the largest we'll ever find will be closer to a mere 50 billion or so.

The discrepancy boils down to just how close an object must get to a black hole to be pulled in. Even the largest black holes are only a few tens of billions of kilometers across—on a similar scale as the size of our solar system—which is tiny on the cosmic stage. From a distance, you're perfectly safe from their gravity. If a solar-mass black hole suddenly replaced our sun, we'd have fatal problems—such as freezing to death—but our falling in wouldn't be one of them; Earth and the other planets would continue in their orbits as if nothing had changed. Similarly, our Milky Way galaxy has a central supermassive black hole called Sagittarius A* that's about four million solar masses. It's some 26,000 light-years away from us, but it causes us no distress at all.

Really, it's rather rare for anything to fall into a black hole—and even when it happens, the mechanics aren't straightforward. Most material won't plunge headlong into the cosmic dumpster's maw. Instead its orbital speed will increase as it falls toward the black hole so that it whirls madly around the compact object. This captive matter will form a flattened disk called an accretion disk.

Within the disk, material closer in will orbit faster than matter farther out. This rotation generates incredible friction, heating the disk to millions of degrees. Matter that hot glows fiercely, which is one way we can detect black holes in the first place: although they're invisible, the effect they have on nearby material can be seen, even clear across the universe, as with 3C 273.

A disk can be so hot that material within it can actually be blown away by the intense radiation. Disks can have powerful magnetic fields that can also draw matter away. Together these effects limit how rapidly a black hole can feed: a glut of infalling material can cause a disk to get so big and hot that it repels any additional approaching matter. This is called the Eddington limit; think of it as how rapidly a black hole can eat without–and pardon the indelicacy, but an analogy is an analogy–vomiting things back out.

So it takes time for a black hole to grow. And time is limited: the universe had a finite beginning. At best a black hole has had 13.8 billion years–the age of the cosmos–to stuff itself. And the earliest evidence we've found for black holes dates to a few hundred million years after that time, further limiting their cosmic feeding frenzy.

Factoring in these temporal limitations, we can conclude that the biggest black hole today should be no larger than 270 billion times the mass of the sun. And that's only if all its feedstock is revolving in the same direction as the black hole's spin, which acts as a digestive aid, allowing material to fall in more rapidly. If the black hole doesn't spin or the material falls in the direction opposite to that spin, the upper limit falls to the 50-billion-solar-mass figure.

This smaller number is indeed in the ballpark of the highest black hole masses we have detected. Some black holes, such as one called TON 618, appear to be a bit bigger, but there is a lot of uncertainty in that number, and the lower limit is probably a little fuzzy as well.

I hasten to add that despite all this detailed discussion of how black holes dine on matter, they can also grow a different way, via cosmic cannibalism: when galaxies collide, their individual supermassive black holes can eventually fall together and merge to become a single, even bigger black hole. That's a time-saver! But really huge black holes are so rare—never mind the even rarer prospect of their merging—that it's unlikely this phenomenon would significantly expand the boundaries on black hole growth.

So we don't expect to find one any more massive than those we've already managed to measure. But the universe is smarter than we are, and it's still possible an even more colossal black hole might exist. If that is the case, astronomers will have a chance to do their favorite thing: go back to their assumptions and try to figure out what they missed, learning more about these behemoths in the process. In that way, our knowledge grows, and there's no upper limit to that.

About the Author

Phil Plait is a professional astronomer and science communicator in Virginia. His column for Scientific American, *The Universe, covers all things space. He writes the* Bad Astronomy Newsletter. *Follow him online.*

Hypervelocity Stars Hint at a Supermassive Black Hole Right Next Door

By Phil Plait

An astonishing fact known for only the past few decades is that every big galaxy in the universe has a supermassive black hole at its heart. Scientists suspected this was the case in the 1980s, and observations from the Hubble Space Telescope, which has peered deep into the cores of galaxies all across the sky, confirmed it. The "normal" kinds of black holes made when stars explode range from five to about 100 times the mass of our sun, more or less. But the central galactic monsters are millions of times more massive, and some have grown to the Brobdingnagian heft of billions of solar masses.

A lot of mysteries remain, of course, such as how these black holes formed early in the history of the universe, how they grew so humongous so fast and what role they played in their host galaxy's formation. One odd question in particular nags at astronomers: What's the galaxy-size cutoff where this trend stops? In other words, is there some lower limit to how massive a galaxy can be and still harbor one of these beasts?

The inklings of an answer are emerging from a surprising place: studies of rare stars moving through our galaxy at truly ludicrous speeds.

Orbiting the Milky Way is a menagerie of smaller "dwarf" galaxies, some so tiny and faint that you need huge telescopes to see them at all. But two are so large and close that they're visible to the unaided eye from the Southern Hemisphere: the Large and Small Magellanic Clouds. The Large Magellanic Cloud (LMC) is the bigger and closer of the two, and it's not clear whether it harbors a supermassive black hole (SMBH). If an SMBH exists there, it must be quiescent, meaning it's not actively feeding on matter. As material falls toward such a black hole, it forms a swirling disk of superheated plasma that can glow so brightly it outshines all the stars in the galaxy combined. No such fierce luminescence is seen in the LMC, so we don't know whether an SMBH is there and not actively feeding or the LMC is simply SMBH-free.

But a recent study published in the *Astrophysical Journal* offers strong evidence that an SMBH does lie at the center of the LMC—based on measurements of stellar motions in our own Milky Way. The study looked at hypervelocity stars, which are screaming through space at speeds far higher than those of stars around them. Some of these stars are moving so rapidly that they have reached galactic escape velocity; the Milky Way's gravity can't hold them. In the coming eons, they'll flee the galaxy entirely. And we have good reason to believe these runaway stars were launched by SMBHs—but how?

Such a situation starts with two stars orbiting each other in a binary system. These systems contain a substantial amount of orbital energy, which is the sum of the kinetic energy of the two stars, or their energy of motion, and their gravitational potential energy, or the amount of energy that would be released if they were to move closer together.

If the binary star approaches a third object, some of that energy can be moved around. One star can become bound to the third object, for instance, whereas the other star gets a boost in its kinetic energy that flings it away. The strength of the kick depends in part on the gravity of the third object. A massive black hole, of course, has an incredibly strong gravitational field that can fling the star away at high speed.

And I do mean at high speed—such a star can be shot from the black hole at a velocity greater than 1,000 kilometers per second. S5-HVS1 was the first confirmed such hypervelocity star, and it's moving at more than 1,700 kilometers per second. Feel free to take a moment to absorb that fact: *an entire star* has been ejected from a black hole at more than six million kilometers per hour. The energies involved are terrifying.

We have seen a few of these stars in our galaxy, and careful measurements suggest they're moving away from the center of the Milky Way, which is pretty convincing evidence that Sagittarius A*, the Milky Way's SMBH, is to blame.

But not all the high-velocity stars that have been detected appear to come from our galactic center. Fortunately, Gaia, a sadly now decommissioned European Space Agency astronomical observatory, was designed to obtain extremely accurate measurements of the positions, distances, colors, and other characteristics—including velocity—of well more than a billion stars.

There are 21 known hypervelocity stars at the outskirts of the Milky Way. Using the phenomenally high-precision Gaia measurements, the astronomers behind the new research examined the stars' three-dimensional velocities through space. They found that five of them have ambiguous origins, and two definitely come from the center of the Milky Way. Of the 14 left, three clearly come from the direction of the LMC.

These stars' trajectories effectively point back to their origins, and based on our current knowledge, those origins must be supermassive black holes. Even better, although the trajectories of the remaining 11 stars are consistent with both Milky Way and LMC origins, the researchers found that five of the stars are more likely to have come from our home galaxy, and the other six are more likely to have come from the LMC.

So there could be nine known hypervelocity stars plunging through our galaxy that were ejected by a supermassive black hole in another galaxy.

Using some sophisticated math, the team found that the most likely mass of the black hole is 600,000 or so times the mass of the sun. This isn't huge for an SMBH—in fact, it's very much on the low end of the scale—but then, the LMC is a small galaxy with a mass only about 1 percent of the Milky Way's. We know that the mass of a black hole tends to scale with its host galaxy's mass (because they form together and affect each other's growth), so this lower mass is consistent with that relation.

If this calculation is accurate, then our satellite galaxy is shooting stars at us! And maybe more have yet to be found, hurtling through space unseen on the other side of our galaxy or so far out that they're difficult to spot and even harder to study. All this information helps us get a clearer—but still quite hazy—sense of just how far down the galactic scale we can expect to find big black holes.

Black holes are funny. Most people would worry about falling into one, among a host of other terrors, but now you can add "having to dodge intergalactic stellar bullets" to that list.

About the Author

Phil Plait is a professional astronomer and science communicator in Virginia. His column for Scientific American, *The Universe, covers all things space. He writes the* Bad Astronomy Newsletter. *Follow him online.*

3,000-Light-Year-Long Jet Offers New Clues to First Black Hole Ever Imaged

By Jackie Flynn Mogensen

Located at the center of the galaxy Messier 87 (M87), the supermassive black hole M87* holds a special place in the science history books: it's the first black hole ever imaged and is the origin of what NASA has called "one of nature's most amazing phenomena." That's because the black hole is spewing out a gigantic jet of material that is blazing a 3,000-light-year-long trail through the cosmos.

M87* is both a messy and greedy eater: as dust and gas falls toward it, the black hole shoots out powerful jets of charged particles. But astronomers didn't exactly know where these jets originated—until now. In new research published in the journal Astronomy & Astrophysics, scientists lay out evidence of what they believe are the "first hints" of M87*'s jet base.

Using observations from the Event Horizon Telescope, the team examined the glowing ring of superhot material around M87* and identified what they believe is the "probable position" of the extremely long jet's origin.

The results could inform future studies of M87*'s superlative jet and the mechanics of similar supermassive black holes.

"This study represents an early step toward connecting theoretical ideas about jet launching with direct observations," said the paper's lead author Saurabh, a researcher at the Max Planck Institute for Radio Astronomy in Bonn, Germany, in a statement.

"Identifying where the jet may originate and how it connects to the black hole's shadow, adds a key piece to the puzzle and points toward a better understanding of how the central engine operates," he said.

About the Author

Jackie Flynn Mogensen is a breaking news reporter at Scientific American. *Before joining* SciAm, *she was a science reporter at* Mother Jones, *where she received a National Academies Eric and Wendy Schmidt Award for Excellence in Science Communications in 2024. Mogensen holds a master's degree in environmental communication and a bachelor's degree in earth sciences from Stanford University. She is based in New York City.*

Back From the Dead, a Black Hole is Erupting After a 100-Million-Year Hiatus

By K. R. Callaway

Inside an incredibly bright cluster of galaxies, a long-dormant supermassive black hole has come back to life. Radio images captured a one-million-light-year-long stream of star-forming particles and gas emanating from the black hole at the center of the galaxy J1007+3540–which apparently is erupting for the first time in about 100 million years.

"Although some 'restarted' radio galaxies are known in the literature, J1007+3540 stands out," says lead study author Shobha Kumari of Midnapore City College in India. The result recently appeared in the *Monthly Notices of the Royal Astronomical Society.*

J1007+3540 is an uncommonly large example of an episodic galaxy, wherein a central supermassive black hole only intermittently emits prominent jets of particles and gas, almost as if an astrophysical on-off switch was flipped. Researchers say the information they gain from the eruption of this "cosmic volcano" could help them better understand episodic galaxies' structures, evolution and influence on their surroundings.

Ejected jets are a consistent but not ubiquitous feature of the supermassive black holes at the hearts of galaxies, which, when erupting, are also called active galactic nuclei (AGNs). Many AGNs are thought to be episodic, ebbing as they exhaust surrounding reservoirs of gas, only to surge again when more material drifts within reach. This cycle elapses across thousands of years–glacially slow to us but almost instantaneous on cosmic scales.

That makes episodic activity and the on-off transition difficult to catch as it occurs. Rather than attempting to observe the changes themselves, scientists often analyze the structures within galaxies they think arise from a central black hole's episodic outbursts. If the black hole is dormant, they look for echoes of its past active phase, such as high-energy light or ionized gas that has traveled farther out from the galaxy's center. And, of course, if a galaxy's central black hole is in its AGN phase, like J1007+3540's, the evidence is obvious.

The radio images of J1007+3540–taken using interferometers at the Low Frequency Array in the Netherlands and the upgraded Giant Meterwave Radio Telescope in India–capture both phases in a single target. The galaxy sports not only a bright newborn jet but also a surrounding surfeit of older material blasted out by past AGN episodes. While other episodic galaxies are expected to have similar structures, J1007+3540's are especially clear.

"This system is just physically very large, and that makes it more amenable to study in many ways," explains Niel Brandt, an astrophysicist at Pennsylvania State University. "You can go in and study it in considerable detail."

One of these details, a faint, fragmented tail of old material extending out into intergalactic space stirred by subsequent outbursts to shine anew, shows how J1007+3540's AGN phase can impact its cosmic neighborhood–specifically, the gas pervading the galaxy cluster where J1007+3540 resides, known as the intracluster medium (ICM). The shape and brightness of the rekindled tail trace the complex interactions that occurred between the AGN's ejected jet and the ICM as the jet propagated outward.

"These observations help us understand that the relationship between a galaxy's jets and the cluster environment is very dynamic," says Vivian U, an astronomer at the Infrared Processing and Analysis Center at the California Institute of Technology.* "The jets don't just carve a path through empty space–they are constantly shaped and changed by the gas they encounter."

There is still a lot left to learn about how interactions with the ICM can feedback to change the form and behavior of a galaxy's jets, all of which can spark (or suppress) the creation of new generations of stars. Somehow the flicker and flutter of AGN at the hearts of galaxies may dictate whether they shine for eons or fade to starless black.

"The oddballs are exciting," says Phil Hopkins, a theoretical astrophysicist at the California Institute of Technology. Observing unusual cases like J1007+3540 gives researchers the opportunity to test and improve their models of how this majestic process unfolds.

About the Author

K. R. Callaway is an editorial intern at Scientific American. *She specializes in science, health, history and policy.*

"Little Red Dots" Spied by JWST May Be Baby Black Holes in Disguise

By Lee Billings

For the past few years, astronomers have grappled with a cosmic enigma first revealed by NASA's James Webb Space Telescope (JWST). Practically everywhere JWST looked in the sky's distant depths, probing a time when our universe was only several hundred million years old, it saw something hard to explain: bright, curiously compact specks that were ruby red. The spots were ubiquitous in scenes from this early epoch. But then, circa two billion years into the universe's history, they vanished from JWST's view just as inexplicably as they appeared.

Further investigations of these "little red dots" (LRDs) deepened the mystery. They looked far too massive and mature to be early galaxies brightened by swarms of newborn stars, yet they weren't blasting out the x-rays and radio waves that are the hallmarks of supermassive black holes feeding on gas and dust. For a time, the LRDs were framed as breaking cosmology because they defied practically every expectation set by well-founded theories.

Now, however, an answer may be at hand. Published on Wednesday in *Nature* and derived from deeper, more time-consuming JWST observations of a dozen LRDs that split their light into its constituent colors, or spectra, a new study strengthens the case that these objects are, in fact, gigantic, growing black holes. If so, the seemingly missing x-ray and radio outbursts from these objects would be cloaked behind dense cocoons of ionized gas. Feeding black holes also usually emit copious ultraviolet radiation from the white-hot disks of material that pile up around their insatiable maws. For the LRDs, that ultraviolet light would filter through their cocoons, trickling out as visible light and creating the characteristic red hue. The LRDs would naturally fade away as the growing, gas-guzzling black holes hollowed out their cocoons.

If confirmed by additional data, this picture could mean that LRDs represent a new, previously unknown phase in the lives of supermassive black holes–and the youngest stage at which we've ever seen them.

"This cocoon makes these black holes look red and prevents much of their radiation from escaping and explains why they look so compact," says the study's lead author Vadim Rusakov, an astrophysicist at the University of Manchester in England. In this scenario, besides disguising the black holes, the cocoons also make these objects appear heavier because electrons from their shrouds of ionized gas scatter outgoing light in a way that mimics the light we see from more massive objects. Correcting for this effect, the research team calculated that the black holes hidden within the LRDs ranged between 100,000 and 10 million solar masses–relative pipsqueaks compared with more mature supermassive black holes, which can tip the cosmic scales at billions of solar masses. "The detailed physics inside the gas cocoon is still an open area of research," Rusakov says. "But we now think the main mystery is solved: LRDs almost certainly host growing black holes."

Not all astronomers are certain the case is closed, however. Of the myriad LRDs glimpsed with JWST, the *Nature* study only closely examines a dozen. It's possible that further observations of many more LRDs could show they aren't all one type of object–perhaps some are cocooned black holes, as the study suggests, and others are different things altogether.

Rodrigo Nemmen, an astrophysicist at the University of São Paulo, who authored an accompanying commentary on the *Nature* study, largely agrees with Rusakov and his team's interpretation. The team's work is "a major step forward," presenting a model that's "elegant and ties up a lot of loose ends," he says. "LRDs once seemed to demand either impossibly efficient galaxy formation or implausibly massive black holes appearing out of nowhere in the young universe–either way, something was badly wrong with our models." But with their estimated masses downsized per the Nature study, any black holes within LRDs would be easier for preexisting models to account for.

These conclusions aren't entirely surprising, notes Rohan Naidu, an astrophysicist at the Massachusetts Institute of Technology, who also studies LRDs. On the same day in March 2025, a preprint version of the *Nature* study was posted online, as were preprints of two other investigations that focused on LRDs—one that was led by Naidu and another that was led by Anna de Graaff of the Center for Astrophysics | Harvard & Smithsonian. All three papers presented complementary results that suggested that LRDs are cocooned supermassive black holes. Additional work from theorists around the globe has further reinforced the idea.

Like many of his peers, Naidu is now so confident in the interpretation that he prefers to call LRDs "black hole stars," because of some of the associated physics. "They effectively radiate like enormous stars," he says, although LRDs can be a trillion times more luminous. "Instead of nuclear fusion holding up the ball of gas like in our sun, we ... have a furiously feeding black hole whose radiation powers this structure."

Yet despite the emerging consensus, key questions remain unanswered.

The crux of contention, Nemmen says, is just how much ionized gas a cocoon would hold and thus how much electron scattering would interfere with the measurement of a lurking black hole's actual mass. Interpreting JWST's spectral data, he says, is "notoriously tricky business," wherein even minor changes could cause the resulting mass estimates to shift significantly—in principle, diminishing them so much that the case for hidden black holes would weaken.

But such an outcome seems unlikely, Rusakov says, given the multiple, independent lines of supporting evidence, as well as the lack of any other plausible mechanism that allows all the various pieces of the LRDs puzzle to fit neatly together. "Without the ionized gas, the data simply don't make sense," he says.

And even if the LRDs mystery has been solved—and cosmology's reigning paradigm saved—a host of new questions would arise. "Can we find even smaller black holes [in the early universe] with JWST? Do they start tiny and grow, or are they born already quite big?" Rusakov asks. "LRDs might be our best candidates to find out."

About the Author

Lee Billings is a science journalist specializing in astronomy, physics, planetary science, and spaceflight and is senior desk editor for physical science at Scientific American. *He is author of a critically acclaimed book,* Five Billion Years of Solitude: The Search for Life Among the Stars, *which in 2014 won a Science Communication Award from the American Institute of Physics. In addition to his work for* Scientific American, *Billings's writing has appeared in the* New York Times, *the* Wall Street Journal, *the* Boston Globe, Wired, New Scientist, Popular Science *and many other publications. Billings joined Scientific American in 2014 and previously worked as a staff editor at* SEED *magazine. He holds a B.A. in journalism from the University of Minnesota.*

Could Colossal Black Hole Jets Have Shaped the Early Universe?

By Saima S. Iqbal

In a galaxy 7.5 billion light-years away, a supermassive black hole shoots out streams of magnetized plasma that span 140 Milky Ways in length. This mind-boggling structure–nicknamed Porphyrion, after a giant from Greek mythology–contains the largest black hole jets physicists have ever seen, a team reported in *Nature* last month. And its existence suggests that black hole jets may have played a more important role in shaping the cosmos than previously thought.

Black holes occasionally generate jets when they overeat, as matter piles up around their maw and encounters extreme astrophysical forces. All matter that approaches a black hole takes on the form of a spiraling disk. This disk whirls around at such a rapid pace that the material within it glows white-hot and ionizes, transforming into a dense plasma roiling with magnetic fields. A spinning black hole can then twist these magnetic fields into tight cones at each of its rotational poles. Most matter exiting the disk will speed straight into the mouth of the black hole. But a small fraction instead is caught in the twisting fields and slingshots outwards, producing two straight beams that some astrophysicists liken to Jedi lightsabers.

Such jets initially captured scientists' attention because they served as visual markers for black holes, bottomless pits that are otherwise invisible to most telescopes. Only over time did researchers see the jets as important in their own right: the intense heat the streams gave off sometimes prevented surrounding gas from collapsing and forming into new stars. Such an impact, however, seemed limited because the jets were thought not to stretch too far beyond the confines of their own galaxy, if at all. The sky survey that underpins the new study has complicated that picture by identifying more than 10,000 massive black hole jet systems, chief among them Porphyrion.

Streams as ancient and colossal as Porphyrion may have contributed to some of the early universe's features, says lead study author Martijn Oei, an astronomer at the California Institute of Technology.

In 2022 Oei and his fellow researchers uncovered another black-hole-spewing jet system that, end-to-end, spans 16 million light-years, or 100 Milky Ways. Porphyrion beats out this previous record holder, Alcyoneus, not only with its absolute size but also with its relative influence on its cosmic surroundings. Born when the universe was less than half its current age and thereby much smaller and denser than it is today, Porphyrion can reach out and touch more than Alcyoneus ever could.

Porphyrion's jets are estimated to contain the total power of trillions of suns and raise the temperature of surrounding gas by a million degrees Celsius. This means they may have inhibited the formation of not just stars but entire galaxies in the early universe. Their high-speed sprays of magnetized ejecta also could have pierced and filled voids in the cosmic web, the network of matter-rich filaments and matter-sparse cavities that forms the universe's large-scale structure.

Oei is most intrigued by the possibility that jet systems like Porphyrion may have helped set the stage for life on Earth. Our planet's magnetic field shields Earth's biosphere and atmosphere from barrages of high-energy cosmic rays and dangerous outbursts of solar particles and radiation. Yet Earth's magnetic field is itself embedded in and therefore interlinked with the magnetic field of our star, which in turn lies within other magnetic fields stretching across the Milky Way–and perhaps even beyond. This scalar trail is long and tenuous, but it may trace all the way back through time and space to our own perch on a strand of the cosmic web–and to potential perturbations from structures like Porphyrion.

To better assess the impact such jets may have had on the early universe, researchers will need to create a more comprehensive catalog of the structures. The new study surveys just 15 percent of the sky, possibly leaving many more jets yet to be discovered. And it's difficult to estimate how many of these gargantuan structures exist, Oei notes, because the conditions that produce and sustain powerful streams remain poorly understood.

That scientists can even make out such large jets is a testament to the sensitivity of modern telescopes. The sheer size of the jets makes them hard to detect in the small field of view available from most suitably powerful telescopes. In the new study, Oei and his team members turned to a European network of radio telescopes called the Low Frequency Array (LOFAR), searching its images of the sky for radio light with a wavelength of approximately two meters. These "human-sized waves" offered signs of "places where something violent and spectacular happens," he says. When Porphyrion popped up, they used two other facilities–the Giant Metrewave Radio Telescope in India and the W. M. Keck Observatory in Hawaii–to discover and study the galaxy that was the source of the signal. Having initially set out to study the cosmic web, Oei found Porphyrion's pair of jets to be twice the surprise–and he expects countless more as the team continues to study Porphyrion and other systems of gigantic jets.

About the Author

Saima S. Iqbal is a former Scientific American *news intern. She specializes in health and medicine and is based in New York City.*

Weird, Wobbling Black Hole Jets Can Shape Entire Galaxies

By Jacek Krywko

For decades, astronomers have known that supermassive black holes lurk at the hearts of essentially all large galaxies, occasionally feasting on infalling material and burping out powerful jets. But what's been less clear is how, exactly, this activity shapes their surrounding galaxies.

Now researchers have found a crucial piece of this galactic puzzle by observing a supermassive black hole shooting out a wobbling jet in the galaxy VV 340A, some 450 million light-years from Earth. The jet acts as a cosmic scale snowplow, pushing away gas that would otherwise fuel the creation of new stars. The result was announced at this year's winter meeting of the American Astronomical Society in Phoenix, Ariz.

"Conventionally, there are two modes of gas outflows driven by supermassive black holes in galaxies," says Justin Kader, an astrophysicist at the University of California, Irvine and first author of an associated paper published in *Science*. In the first so-called radiative mode, a white-hot, incandescent accretion disk of infalling matter forms around a rapidly feeding supermassive black hole, heating the nearby gas. This heated gas then expands and pushes the cooler gas outward. "You can see the gas flowing out of the galaxy in these wide-angle bicone structures," Kader explains.

In the second jet-driven mode, a black hole launches firehoselike jets of particles and radiation from its poles, kinetically pushing surrounding gas far out of the galaxy. These jets, though, usually add to a galaxy's stellar inventory as they jostle and compress gas clouds that then gravitationally collapse to churn out more stars.

In VV 340A, however, Kader and his colleagues found jets from a supermassive black hole doing something distinctly different from either of these two modes.

VV 340A is a spiral galaxy that is merging with another, VV 340B, forming a system collectively called VV 340. In the sky, the pair appear as a celestial exclamation point, with VV 340B's disk oriented face-on as the exclamation point's "dot" and VV 340A's edge-on disk forming the "dash." For Kader and his colleagues, this edge-on orientation was a stroke of luck, allowing them to more easily probe the inner workings of VV 340A. What they found shooting out of the galaxy's central black hole wasn't a standard, straight jet. Instead it was an enigmatic S-shaped structure, demanding deeper investigation to determine its nature.

Using the infrared eyes of the James Webb Space Telescope, the team could pierce the thick dust veiling VV 340A's center to discover a massive cloud of superheated, ionized plasma stretching out for nearly 20,000 light-years—far larger than any other black-hole-generated plasma cloud ever seen. Subsequent optical observations at the Keck Observatory in Hawaii confirmed this ionized plasma wasn't just sitting still but was propelled outward at immense speeds. Finally, radio observations of VV 340A via two radio telescopes, the Karl G. Jansky Very Large Array and the Atacama Large Millimeter Array, showed the plasma was perfectly aligned with the S-shaped jet coming from the black hole.

Kader and his co-authors think this S shape is the hallmark of precession, the same wobble you see in a spinning top as it slows down or in water spewing from the rotating head of a lawn sprinkler. As the black hole spins, its jet doesn't just point in one direction—it sweeps through space in a conical motion, pushing the star forming gas out of the galaxy at a rate of around 20 solar masses per year. That's enough, the researchers estimate, to shorten VV 340A's star-forming lifespan by about 250 million years.

"Twenty solar masses per year is no big deal," says Andrew Fabian, a British astronomer and former director of the Institute of Astronomy at the University of Cambridge, who was not involved in the study. "But a precessing jet as the driver of gas outflow is something new. It does indeed show that it can significantly move matter around in a spiral galaxy." One of the still unanswered questions for Kader and his colleagues is what exactly causes the jet's wobbling motion.

"These wobbling jets are not common, but they have been observed before, mostly in giant elliptical galaxies," Kader says, noting there are presently thought to be two main drivers for the behavior. One is an accretion disk instability, in which a large clump of gas falling toward the black hole tugs on the disk of material surrounding it, causing it to tilt.

The other, arguably more exciting possibility is that there isn't just one black hole at the center of the VV 340A but two. A binary pair of supermassive black holes orbiting each other could gravitationally whip the jet around like a garden hose. "To the best of my knowledge, a binary supermassive black hole has not been ever directly observed before. We do not claim we observed that, but it's one of two possible options," Kader says.

Higher-resolution radio observations, paired with studies using future observatories such as NASA's Nancy Grace Roman Space Telescope, could help discern between these two possibilities. In the meantime, the team has flagged another 32 galaxies that are similar to VV 340A for further scrutiny. "What we want to see is the interaction of different gases in the galaxy merger process", says study co-author Vivian U, also at the University of California, Irvine. "Being able to understand that would allow us to actually answer one of those big-picture questions–to understand the drivers of galaxies' growth."

About the Author

Jacek Krywko is a freelance writer who covers space exploration, artificial intelligence, computer science and all sorts of engineering wizardry.

Our Galaxy's Biggest Black Hole Just Got a New Close-up. What's Next Could Be Even Wilder

By Michael Greshko

At the center of our galaxy lurks a dark, beating heart: Sagittarius A*, a black hole some four million times more massive than our sun. We cannot see this fearsome object directly—only its shadow, a lightless bubble nestled within an "accretion disk" of infalling incandescent plasma. Spotting this light-ringed dark orb from our place in the Milky Way's hinterlands is almost unfathomably difficult, like spotting a single virus particle that's half a mile away.

But thanks to a global network of radio observatories called the Event Horizon Telescope (EHT), scientists can not only glimpse this glowing doughnut but also map its monstrous magnetic fields. Yet as remarkable as these observations may be, they pale in comparison to what some astronomers hope to see a decade from now with an upgraded EHT.

Black holes are among the most enigmatic and important characters in our great cosmic drama. Whether they form from a single star or weigh in at billions of stellar masses, they are thought to power many of the most energetic phenomena in the known universe, from quasars to gamma-ray bursts. And supermassive black holes play a huge role in shaping the structure and flow of matter within their home galaxies. As a supermassive black hole accretes matter, the energy released in the form of high-energy radiation can heat up and redistribute the surrounding gas—affecting, among other things, galactic rates of star formation. "They are literally the origin of life, in a way," says Sara Issaoun, a postdoctoral fellow at the Center for Astrophysics | Harvard & Smithsonian (CfA).

But so far, only two black holes have made it into the EHT's high-resolution photo album: Sagittarius A* and the even larger M87*, a 6.5-billion-solar-mass gargantuan at the center of Messier

87, or M87, a giant elliptical galaxy some 55 million light-years from Earth. The first snapshot came in 2019 when the EHT released an image of the plasmatic torus encircling M87*. In 2022 the EHT followed suit with Sagittarius A*. These breakthrough observations sparked deeper looks: in 2021 researchers announced that they had measured how light is polarized across M87*'s inner accretion disk, which let them chart the magnetic fields around the black hole. Now the EHT team has done the same for Sagittarius A* and detailed its results in twostudies recently published in the *Astrophysical Journal Letters*.

"Imagine you're at the beach, and you look out and you want to go swimming. If you don't see the undertow, you can be in a lot of trouble," says CfA astrophysicist Shep Doeleman, EHT's founding director. "The polarization lets us see the structure below the glow that we've been seeing."

The thousandfold mass difference between Sagittarius A* and M87* explains why the latter's magnetic underpinnings were seen first. Because our own galaxy's central black hole is roughly a thousand times less massive than M87*, the churning maelstrom around Sagittarius A* can change about a thousand times faster, too: features that may persist for days around M87* can come and go in mere minutes around Sagittarius A*. That transience made getting a sharp long-exposure image of the black hole over several hours especially tricky. "Sagittarius A* is such a problem-child black hole," says Issaoun, who led the observational side of the analysis. "We were very concerned about being able to get an image at all. But it was actually pretty surprising; the polarization data ended up being a lot calmer than we had predicted."

Despite the differences in mass and M87*'s prominent, iconic jet, the polarized light detected by the EHT around each supermassive black hole shows a striking similarity with profound implications: both boast accretion disks shaped by strong, ordered magnetic fields. "I'm quite excited," says Alex Chen, a theoretical astrophysicist at Washington University in St. Louis, who is not a member of the

EHT Collaboration. "This is a very, very interesting result that humanity has not been able to get–like, ever."

And as the EHT pursues an ambitious upgrade plan, this surprising result may prove to be only the opening chapter of a grander tale that will reveal the quirks of the giant gravitational beasts lurking within the Milky Way, M87 and a host of other nearby large galaxies.

SANE or MAD?

Collectively, the EHT's studies to date point toward an answer to a longstanding debate in astrophysics: Do the accretion flows around black holes tend to be SANE, or are they MAD?

Under the SANE (standard and normal evolution) model of accretion flows, magnetic fields around a black hole are relatively weak and constantly jostled by swirling, turbulent plasma within the accretion disk. In MAD (magnetically arrested disk) models, however, magnetic fields can be stronger and play a dominant role in shaping a black hole's accretion disk, corralling the plasma into more orderly arrangements.

"It's almost a little bit like watching a waterfall," Doeleman says. "Sometimes when the conditions are just right, you'll get this nice smooth flow of water over the waterfall. It'll almost seem glassy. And then you'll also see, with different conditions, turbulent flow with a lot of bubbles in it."

These two different models each imply a different, distinctive polarization signature. Most of the glow that the EHT is picking up from the edges of Sagittarius A* and M87* is generated by what's called synchrotron emission. As charged particles rapidly gyrate around the magnetic field lines around the black hole, they emit linearly polarized photons–and the specific pattern of those photons' polarization angles depends on the structure of the underlying magnetic field lines. In the case of MAD, the polarization angles should reveal a majestic spiraling symmetry to the magnetic field. If SANE ruled the day, the polarization angles would be more scrambled. For both M87* and Sagittarius A*, the EHT's polarization data suggest a highly ordered magnetic structure, favoring the MAD model.

That swing in MAD's favor also hints at something interesting about Sagittarius A* and thus about the Milky Way: its likelihood of sporting black hole–powered jets like its larger cousin.

In computer simulations, black holes with MAD-like magnetic fields are particularly efficient at generating huge jets of charged particles, like the cosmic blowtorch that stretches out for thousands of light-years from M87*. Thanks to what's known as the Blandford–Znajek mechanism, a spinning black hole wreathed by a strongly magnetized accretion disk can drag along the magnetic field lines threaded into it. This process creates two spiraling cones of magnetic field lines over the black hole's poles like the twisted ends of a candy wrapper. Charged particles can then accelerate along these field lines up and away from the black hole, forming jets in the process.

But if Sagittarius A* has or once had such jets, astronomers have yet to conclusively see them. Instead they've surmised their possible existence from multiple lines of circumstantial evidence. Two vast plasma structures aglow with high-energy gamma rays, known as the Fermi bubbles, extend above and below the plane of the Milky Way in mute testament to past tumult in the galactic center. X-ray and radio images of our galaxy's core reveal large-scale filaments of magnetized plasma. One study published last year in the *Astrophysical Journal Letters* analyzed the orientations of these filaments and found subtle hints of a jetlike outflow emanating from Sagittarius A* through the Milky Way's starry disk.

At present, the EHT can't see the jet of M87*, let alone any similar feature from Sagittarius A*. That's because such jets are undetectably dim at the radio wavelengths used by the EHT—for now, anyway. The EHT team is lobbying for its ambitious plan to upgrade its facilities during the coming decade and radically transform our up-close views of black holes. "We're really excited to see if this jet is really there," Issaoun says. "I think we'd be able to see it."

The Next Generation

The next-generation Event Horizon Telescope, or ngEHT for short, would add a dedicated network of approximately 10 new antennas to the collaboration's existing international array.

The EHT team assembles its unique images by combining the data from a global network of millimeter-wave telescopes all looking for days on end at the same supermassive black hole. Through clever and intensive data processing that compares slight variations in the signals from each telescope in the network, the EHT effectively becomes a radio antenna the diameter of Earth. Although this virtual Earth-size telescope has astounding angular resolution, the vastness of intergalactic space serves as a spoiler–in its present form the EHT can only probe the black holes of our galaxy and of M87; all others in galaxies with favorable "disk-on" (rather than "edge-on") alignments are too far away to be resolved. Additionally, the EHT's images are effectively monochrome–limited to a small swath of radio wavelengths–and the project can't easily monitor its targets for extended periods.

The new antennas would roughly double the number of participating telescopes, while also adding upgrades that let the EHT observe at two or possibly three different radio frequencies at once. A more broadband radio view of black holes in multicolor would be a scientific boon because it would let astronomers tease out certain effects of magnetic fields (which vary by frequency) and Einstein's general relativity (which don't) in exquisite detail. Adding multiple frequencies alone would improve ngEHT's resolution by up to 50 percent over today's EHT, according to a paper published last October in the journal *Galaxies*. In all, the ngEHT is aiming for a resolution of 15 microarcseconds: good enough to spot a single virus particle from more than three quarters of a mile away.

These upgrades would also greatly expand the number of black holes the EHT could meaningfully resolve from only two up to a few dozen or so. It could even spot two black holes at once. Years-long tracking of pulsars across the night sky strongly suggest that spacetime hums with a coffee-shop murmur of gravitational waves given off by pairs of supermassive black holes spiraling into each other in the center of distant galaxies. In principle, ngEHT could spatially resolve such a pair—and see two dark dots instead of one.

In addition, the team envisions using ngEHT to make "movies" of M87* and Sagittarius A*, which would still be, by far, the most favorable targets. "We want these black holes to be, for black hole astrophysics, as useful as the sun is for stellar astrophysics," says CfA postdoctoral fellow Angelo Ricarte, who led the theory side of the new results mapping Sagittarius A*'s magnetic fields. "We want to understand these so well that we can use them as a baseline for other systems."

Since 2019 the ngEHT effort has received more than $14.6 million from the U.S. National Science Foundation (NSF) to fund the design of new hardware and upgrades for the current crop of participating telescopes. Last September the Smithsonian Astrophysical Observatory selected mtex antenna technology, a German firm, to design, develop and build the necessary next-generation antennas. According to Doeleman, completing ngEHT will cost $88 million over several years, a sum that he and his colleagues requested from the NSF in December.

The NSF has not yet revealed whether it will fund a fully scoped ngEHT. That announcement isn't expected any sooner than October, according to the agency's FY2025 budget request.

The EHT Collaboration has even bigger, longer-term ideas for how to snap the best possible black hole picture. Even the ngEHT can only get so good; its virtual telescope's effective light-gathering power is still limited by our planet's size. To get an even better resolution, the EHT would have to increase its diameter beyond that of Earth's—by putting at least one of its telescopes in space.

An EHT team led by CfA astrophysicist Michael Johnson is exploring a space mission concept known as Black Hole Explorer (BHEX). The idea is to place a satellite in orbit around Earth to act as another node of the EHT array. BHEX would boost the array's overall resolution by a factor of three to five—enough, in principle, to allow scientists to see what's known as a photon ring: a sharp, glowing circle formed by photons that repeatedly circle a black hole before escaping outward to sail across the cosmos.

Optimistic performance projections suggest this space-based expansion to ngEHT could even tease out the photon ring's razor-thin substructures, which arise from variations in the number of orbits that different groups of photons complete around a black hole before escaping.

Such observations would provide extraordinarily strict tests of general relativity while also resolving black holes' behavior as never before. How exactly do accretion disks around black holes behave? How do black holes launch their jets? These questions and more could be answered with ngEHT—revealing one of the universe's most mysterious objects in eye-popping detail.

"When we first launched the EHT, we didn't even know if black holes could be imaged," Doeleman says. "Now that we have spectacularly retired that scientific risk, it's time to take a big step."

About the Author

Michael Greshko is a freelance science journalist based in Washington, D.C., and a former staff science writer at National Geographic. *His work has appeared in the* New York Times, *the* Washington Post, Science, Atlas Obscura, MIT Technology *Review and elsewhere. Follow Greshko on social media here.*

The Milky Way's Central Black Hole May Have Appeared Shockingly Different Just a Few Hundred Years Ago

By Jackie Flynn Mogensen

Supermassive black holes are mysterious bodies. Scientists aren't entirely sure how these beating hearts at the centers of most large galaxies formed. That includes Sagittarius A* (Sgr A*), the supermassive black hole at the center of our own Milky Way galaxy.

Now a new preprint study is shedding light on Sagittarius A* by studying what happens as material falls toward the black hole.

Typically, as dust, gas and other material sink toward a supermassive black hole, the black holes emit an "absolute torrent of light," says Steve DiKerby, a postdoctoral researcher at the department of physics and astronomy at Michigan State University and co-author of the new paper. Sagittarius A*, however, is pretty dim. "It's emitting only a tiny trickle of radiation," DiKerby says.

Yet that wasn't always the case. Rather DiKerby and his colleagues' work suggests that the disk of material swirling around Sagittarius A* once emitted much, much brighter x-rays–as much as 10,000 times brighter than those it emits today. Incredibly, that may have been the case as recently as a few hundred years ago, the research suggests.

The findings were presented at a meeting of the American Astronomical Society earlier this month and have been accepted for publication in *Astrophysical Journal Letters*.

The work is "very important," says Joseph Michail, a postdoc at the Center for Astrophysics | Harvard & Smithsonian. It "tells us about the 'recent' history" of Sagittarius A*–something that had been missing from the research record, he says.

"This work shows something completely different from the Sgr A* we know and love–it was incredibly bright," Michail says.

DiKerby and his colleagues used a powerful new x-ray telescope called XRISM (X-Ray Imaging and Spectroscopy Mission) to look at clouds of molecular gas surrounding the black hole. These clouds are thought to reflect x-rays coming from around the black hole, acting as a "cosmic mirror" into its past, DiKerby explains.

"We can not only know how bright Sagittarius A* is today but also how bright it appeared 100 years ago and 1,000 years ago," he says.

To put its change in brightness into perspective, the brightest observed x-ray flare from Sagittarius A* happened in 2013, but that event had only 1 percent of the brightness of what the black hole may have emitted perhaps as recently as a few hundred years ago, Michail says.

"Effectively, XRISM is telling us that something substantial happened" to the black hole sometime in the past few centuries, Michail says. What, however, remains a mystery–for now.

About the Author

Jackie Flynn Mogensen is a breaking news reporter at Scientific American. *Before joining* SciAm, *she was a science reporter at* Mother Jones, *where she received a National Academies Eric and Wendy Schmidt Award for Excellence in Science Communications in 2024. Mogensen holds a master's degree in environmental communication and a bachelor's degree in earth sciences from Stanford University. She is based in New York City.*

Black Hole Caught Blasting Matter into Space at 130 Million MPH

By Claire Cameron

Supermassive black holes are the monsters of the universe, so it is perhaps only fitting that astronomers discovered one of these behemoths unleashing a bright x-ray flare that one of the researchers, astronomer Matteo Guainazzi, described as "almost too big to imagine" in a European Space Agency (ESA) press release.

Within hours of erupting, the blast faded, and the black hole began to whip up winds more powerful than anything we can imagine on Earth and flinging material into space at about 130 million miles per hour–a fifth of the speed of light. For comparison, plasma ejected during a coronal mass ejection from the sun typically travels at a mere three million mph.

To study the black hole, astronomers used two x-ray space telescopes: the ESA's XMM-Newton and the X-Ray Imaging and Spectroscopy Mission, which is a collaboration between the ESA, NASA and the Japan Aerospace Exploration Agency. Lurking at the center of the spiral galaxy NGC 3783, the supermassive black hole–with a mass of 30 million suns–powers the galaxy's heart, a region known as an active galactic nucleus.

According to Guainazzi's statement, tangled magnetic fields in this region may have suddenly "untwisted," generating the winds. Knowing more about active galactic nuclei, and the way that they generate such powerful jets and winds, is key to understanding how galaxies form and evolve over time, study co-author and ESA researcher fellow Camille Diez said in the press release.

The research was published on Tuesday in *Astronomy & Astrophysics*.

About the Author

Claire Cameron is breaking news chief at Scientific American. *Originally from Scotland, she moved to New York City in 2012. Her work has appeared in* National Geographic, Slate, Inc. Magazine, Nautilus, Semafor, *and elsewhere.*

Section 4: The Stars

When Will We See the Universe's First Stars?

By José María Diego Rodríguez

On Christmas Day 2021, alongside other astronomers, I watched the James Webb Space Telescope (JWST) launch from French Guiana and begin its month-long journey to its destination, 1.5 million kilometers from Earth. The trip was filled with many nerve-racking moments, particularly the week-long period in which the telescope's tennis-court-size sun shield array slowly unfolded like origami from its bus-size liftoff configuration.

Luckily, JWST made the trip safely and began operations in the summer of 2022. Since then, the observatory has started answering some of the biggest questions in astronomy. It's also raised many new ones.

One of the biggest surprises that has emerged is the discovery that supermassive black holes, some with masses more than a million times that of the sun, existed when the universe was no more than about 3 percent of its current age. How such massive black holes came to exist so long ago is a puzzle. Perhaps less massive black holes formed from the explosive deaths of the first stars, known as Population III stars, and those black holes later merged under the influence of gravity to form a million-solar-mass black hole.

But how could thousands of these smaller black holes have combined in the cosmically short period of hundreds of millions of years? To figure it out, we need to understand the very first stars, which, to date, no one has ever seen individually.

Known as dinosaur stars for both their primeval nature and their immense size, Population III stars existed only when the universe was very young. At that time chemistry was simple. The stars would have been made of hydrogen, helium and tiny traces of light elements such as lithium because those were the only elements that existed then.

In such a pristine environment, when the universe was much denser than it is today, much more massive stars were able to form than those we can observe now. Such large stars are the analogues of 20th-century rock stars—or pop stars (pun intended). They lived fast and died young, and like all great rock bands do, they left a mark on the universe. During their short lives, just a few million years long, Population III stars churned out heavier elements such as carbon, oxygen, nitrogen, silicon, sulfur and iron through fusion within their cores. When they died in supernova explosions, those elements poured into the universe and seeded the ingredients that would later be essential to form planets and life as we know it. What was left after one of these supernovae was, in most cases, a black hole.

Scientists have yet to observe Population III stars individually, but that could soon change. Thanks to JWST, along with a helpful boost from nature called gravitational lensing, we might get a glimpse of them as they were during their brief lifetimes or be able to detect their very bright final explosions. We might even see the shining gas around their skeletal black holes, which would appear to us as a small quasar.

It's simply amazing that humans can hope to observe such relics from the very beginning of time. These stars won't just teach us about the early universe—they might also shed light on one of its biggest mysteries: dark matter. The cosmos seems to be filled with invisible matter we don't understand, but the light of the first stars must have traveled through it on the way to our telescopes, so this light can teach us about its nature.

My personal journey to study these early stars started more than 10 years ago, after I had worked on different astronomical questions at several institutes across the U.K., the U.S. and Spain. At that point I temporarily relocated to the U.S. to work with data from the best telescope at the time, NASA's Hubble Space Telescope, and on my favorite topic, gravitational lensing.

As powerful as the Hubble and James Webb telescopes are, they are not large enough to see Population III stars without a boost. Fortunately, the universe has been kind to astronomers and has built thousands of naturally occurring telescopes that magnify the distant galaxies lying behind them. Similar to the way a piece of glass can be turned into a magnifying lens that curves light, very massive objects in the universe can bend space itself. When light travels through this warped space, it also bends. Albert Einstein predicted this molding of space and light, which is known as gravitational lensing.

The most massive objects in the universe, and thus the most powerful natural lenses, are galaxy clusters, swarms of hundreds to thousands of galaxies packed together in a relatively small volume that also contains vast amounts of the mysterious substance called dark matter. Galaxy clusters can have masses up to 1,000 times that of the Milky Way and are held together by gravity. When we point a telescope at one of them, the cluster's gravity both amplifies and distorts our view of the background galaxies, thereby creating the gravitational lens. Light from an object behind the center of the lens will be amplified and distorted into a circular shape called an Einstein ring.

When we point JWST toward a gravitational lens, we are adding an extra giant lens in front of the telescope, effectively transforming the observatory into a cosmic microscope. Gravitational lenses magnify only a small portion of the space behind them, just as microscopes do. And the magnification provided by the gravitational lens is not uniform: most of the area behind the galaxy cluster is magnified by factors of less than 10, but in some very small regions, termed caustics, the effect can be very strong, with magnification factors of up to around 10,000.

If a sufficiently bright but small object happens to be in one of these caustics, we can get an otherwise impossibly zoomed-in view of it. When JWST points at one of them, it acts like a telescope 100 times larger than it is, offering the opportunity to take a very high-resolution peek at the distant universe. The only catch is that the objects we can observe with this technique must be relatively small and bright. Population III stars meet these two requirements.

Astronomers are getting close to scoring front-row seats to these elusive stars. In recent years we have glimpsed some of the most ancient stars yet. In 2016, five years before the launch of JWST, astronomers used the Hubble telescope to spot Icarus, the first star observed through a cosmic microscope. Icarus lies a whopping 200 times farther away than the most distant star known before it.

Patrick Kelly of the University of Minnesota, who led the team that discovered Icarus, named it after the mythological character who flew too close to the sun, in reference to the high magnification that revealed it. The scientists first noticed Icarus because its brightness fluctuated between observations separated by months. Very few objects in the universe exhibit this type of change in brightness; after considering all plausible options, the researchers determined that a blue supergiant star was the only possible candidate that could explain the observations.

The brightness fluctuations were the result of a different lensing effect, microlensing, produced by much smaller masses. For most astrophysical objects, this effect is negligible. But for background stars whose magnification can change considerably in a matter of weeks, such as Icarus, it can lead to dimming and brightening. When a microlens temporarily aligns with a telescope, a galaxy cluster lens and a distant background star, the star's brightness can increase by up to a factor of 10. The alignment tends to last for a few weeks. During microlensing episodes, the background star twinkles in a well-known and predictable way that allows us to recognize it as an individual star.

Microlensing is produced mostly by stars in a galaxy cluster, but it can also arise from small concentrations of mass, including structures composed of dark matter. Microlensing can act as an additional lens in the cosmic microscope, increasing its power even further.

Icarus held the record as the most distant star ever observed for a few years, until the 2022 discovery of Earendel. This star–discovered by a team led by Brian Welch, then at Johns Hopkins University, and Dan Coe of the Space Telescope Science Institute–was found to be five times farther away. Of course, Icarus and Earendel are long gone; we are seeing them as they were billions of years ago because their light has taken that long to reach us. Earendel, for instance, appears as it existed when the universe was 7 percent of its current age. The estimated gravitational lensing magnification for Earendel is close to 10,000 times–the highest magnification observed so far. Earendel is the closest we have come to observing Population III stars, and astronomers think some of these original stars were still around at the time our observations of Earendel represent–so we may soon see them, too. Most likely, however, we will need to observe further back in time to see the first generation of stars.

Recent years have witnessed the discovery of tens of individual stars at extreme cosmic distances. On its journey to us, their light has crossed half the universe and gathered valuable information along the way. This light can tell us, for instance, about dark matter, a substance of unknown composition that permeates the entire cosmos. By far the most abundant form of matter in the universe, dark matter has evaded detection by the most advanced laboratories on Earth. It might be made of particles a tiny fraction of the size of an electron, or it might consist of black holes harboring masses comparable to the sun's. Regardless of what it is, dark matter virtually ignores ordinary matter (and our expensive detectors).

Fortunately for us, lensed stars can help us map the distribution of dark matter and reveal some of its properties. If dark matter in the gravitational lens forms invisible structures with masses comparable to or larger than those of planets, these structures will introduce a small but measurable change in the magnification of the lensed star. My team and I, now based at the Institute of Physics of Cantabria in Spain, have measured this type of anomaly in at least two lensed stars, named Godzilla and Mothra. This research revealed two invisible structures with masses in the range of tens of thousands to hundreds of millions of solar masses. If these structures are dominated by dark matter, they will rule out certain theories of dark matter under which it couldn't form such small structures.

Future observations of these and other lensed stars can tell us more about what dark matter can and can't be.

Perhaps the most spectacular lensed stars we have discovered lie in the Dragon Arc galaxy, the first lensed galaxy ever observed, which was seen in the second half of the 20th century. The Dragon Arc isn't extremely far from us–it's "only" 6.5 billion light-years away. But many areas within the galaxy are magnified by factors exceeding 100, so we see the galaxy as it would look to a telescope 10 times larger than JWST. James Webb observed the Dragon Arc in 2023 and discovered more than 40 individual stars through their twinkles. Some studies of the stars in the galaxy suggest that dark matter may be composed of incredibly small particles, even lighter than the hypothetical axion predicted by quantum chromodynamics, a popular dark matter candidate. These studies also suggest that dark matter may have bizarre quantum properties that scientists call "fuzzy," giving dark matter weird wavelike characteristics. At press time, JWST was poised to observe the Dragon Arc once more in search of new lensed stars to help answer these questions.

Using the latest telescopes along with nature's lenses to observe ancient stars puts us in a new golden era of astronomy. JWST is regularly discovering distant stars, and new observatories are set to join it. NASA's Nancy Grace Roman Space Telescope, to be launched in late 2026, will observe about 12 percent of the sky and should reveal thousands of new lensed galaxies at vast distances. Astronomers will then use JWST to observe the most promising candidates for harboring Population III stars in the hope that we can catch a primordial star near the region of high magnification.

Other space telescopes, such as the European Space Agency's relatively new Euclid observatory, are monitoring even larger areas (about 30 percent of the sky) and are already uncovering myriad new gravitational lenses. Some of these lenses could be the first to reveal Population III stars when reobserved with JWST.

Even more exciting is the potential of a future NASA mission, the Habitable Worlds Observatory (HWO), which will have capabilities surpassing those of JWST in some ways. This supertelescope is still under consideration by NASA, and its final design and specifications have yet to be defined. Already, though, it promises an unparalleled opportunity to see the most distant stars. Many Population III stars, for instance, are thought to be very hot and might be too warm to be detected by JWST, which is better suited for cooler stars.

Our knowledge of the best natural gravitational lenses and the best magnified galaxies to observe will have advanced significantly by the time this new telescope is launched. Perhaps by then the first dinosaur stars will have already been confirmed, and we can study them in greater detail with HWO. These tools should help us extend our frontier even further back in time, closer to the beginning of the cosmos, revealing the universe's first stars as well as our own origins.

About the Author

José María Diego Rodríguez is an astrophysicist at the Spanish National Research Council (CSIC). He studies cosmology and the nature of dark matter.

The Pleiades Star Cluster Has a Secret Stellar Family Scattered across the Milky Way

By Phil Plait

The sun wanders the Milky Way alone; our star orbits the galaxy's distant center without any stellar siblings. But it wasn't always this way. The solar system was very likely born in a tremendous gas cloud that also birthed thousands of other stars, forming a large, loosely bound stellar family called an open cluster.

These stars may have remained enshrouded in that nebula for 10 million years or more, until their combined stellar winds and light pushed away the surrounding nebulosity. No longer embedded in the gas, the cluster gradually disintegrated as its internal motions flung away some of its members. Throw in collisions with other huge clouds of gas and dust, as well as interactions with the galaxy's gravitational field, and the cluster's fate was sealed: its stars dispersed, eventually mixing with the background "field" stars in the Milky Way.

Our solar kin may be long lost, but that's not the case for all stars. Some groupings are younger than the sun's 4.6-billion-year age—and are still in the process of eroding away. Interestingly, we see such loose affiliations of stars (called associations) all over the sky, and they often share similar characteristics, such as age and velocity, through the galaxy. Astronomers now suspect that many of these scattered associations formed in the same gas cloud, where they were born as part of a single, sprawling structure that has since broken up. But we might yet glimpse parts of such long-lost clusters that are still intact because stars from their close-packed cores should be tightly bound to each other via gravity and thus able to survive as a tight-knit group for much longer.

Finding such surviving clusters is important; they can tell us about when and where many of the Milky Way's stars formed and how our galaxy's stellar populations and structures evolved over billions of years. In short, studying these stellar relics can lead to a better perception of the galaxy as a whole.

So where are they?

If you're in the Northern Hemisphere and go outside on a clear winter's night, you might notice a fuzzy clutch of stars not too far from Orion. This is the Pleiades (pronounced "PLEE-uh-deez"), a lovely cluster that is about 440 light-years from Earth and located in the constellation Taurus. Six stars can be seen by the unaided eye, although many cultures' ancient myths indicate there are seven. It's possible two of the stars have moved closer together in the sky over time, making it hard to separate them; we still call these stars the Seven Sisters.

Binoculars reveal many dozens of stars in the Pleiades, and hundreds can be seen in deep astronomical images. The cluster doesn't have a sharp boundary, but most of the stars are found in a volume that is about 40 light-years across.

It's about 125 million years old, give or take several million years. If it was once part of a bigger structure, this estimated age would align with our expectation that that structure's outer stars would have been shaken loose. Could the Pleiades be the leftover core of a long-gone cluster?

Finding any far-flung stars that once were anchored by the Pleiades is not an easy task. The sky is big, and the Pleiades' swath of the Milky Way also contains millions of other stars. Astronomers took this on, however, and published their results on November 12 in the *Astrophysical Journal*.

They were clever, reasoning that any stars that used to hang out with the Pleiades would have similar ages and chemical compositions, and would probably still have close to the same motion through the galaxy, as the cluster's current members. By cross-referencing known Pleiades members and a vast stellar database from the European Space Agency mission Gaia, the team pinpointed a selection of stars hurtling through the Milky Way within five kilometers per second of the galactic velocity of the Pleiades.

To firm up this connection, the researchers next estimated the ages of these stars—a difficult task but one that was made easier by the knowledge that younger stars tend to rotate faster than older ones. (This effect exists because a star's magnetic field can sweep up surrounding material and act like drag on a parachute, slowing the star's spin.) A star's rotation can be determined by looking for tiny variations in brightness as dark star spots—which are like the sun's sunspots but appear on other stars—rotate in and out of view. Using data from NASA's Transiting Exoplanet Survey Satellite, which can precisely measures stellar brightness, the astronomers found stars that rotated with periods shorter than 12 days, which is roughly the expected spin rate for stars as old as the average Pleiades member.

Finally, after applying various statistical techniques to look for other stars, the researchers wound up with a list of more than 10,000 possible members of what they called the Greater Pleiades Complex. Mapping these members in three dimensions, they found that the stars fall in a slightly elongated grouping that is about 1,600 by 2,000 light-years in size. This includes stars that belong to at least seven previously known associations. Among these associations is the AB Doradus group, which contains a few dozen stars that are only about 70 light-years from the sun. Another, called UPK 303, had been proposed to be a "tidal tail" of the Pleiades, stars torn away from the cluster by the galaxy's gravity, and the new study supports that conclusion. In fact, looking at the stars' motions and running the clock backward, the astronomers found that they were all within about 200 light-years of the central Pleiades about 75 million years ago, which is consistent with all of these stars being part of a larger structure that is now well into the process of "evaporating" into the galaxy.

This delights and amazes me. I've had my eye on the Pleiades ever since I first started looking at the sky as a wee lad, and I cannot say how many times I've gawked at them through various telescopes and in dramatic images. If you go out sometime to look at them—and I really hope you do—gaze upon that tight little cluster and consider that there's still so much we don't know about these stars—and so much more they can tell us about the cosmos.

About the Author

Phil Plait is a professional astronomer and science communicator in Virginia. His column for Scientific American, *The Universe, covers all things space. He writes the* Bad Astronomy Newsletter. *Follow him online.*

What's the Most Massive Star in the Universe?

By Phil Plait

It's "common knowledge"–and the scare quotes should be a warning–that the sun is an average star.

But it's not, and in fact it's not even close: The sun is in the top 90th percentile of stars by mass. That's because well more than half of the universe's stars are tiny, cool red dwarfs, dim bulbs with half to less than 10 percent of the sun's mass. The lower limit is around 7 to 8 percent of the sun's mass; any less than that, and there isn't enough pressure in the core to sustain nuclear fusion, which is the prime characteristic of what makes a star a star.

But what about the other end? There are stars *far* beefier than our own. Is there an upper limit to how massive a star can be?

Yes, there is, and we do see some stars edging close to it. If they get too close, however, they produce so much energy that they tear themselves apart. One reason this "too close" region isn't itself the hard limit on stellar mass is because its value has changed over time!

Before we dive into the fun science of all this, let's remember the reasons why mass is what's important here rather than size or weight. Size is a problem because stars lack well-defined surfaces, and this problem gets worse the larger a star gets–the biggest ones are so bloated that they just fade away with distance from their respective centers like clouds of fog. Weight won't work because it's just a second-order measure of mass–or rather how strong the gravitational force is on an object with mass. You have the same mass on Earth as you do on the moon, though you weigh differently because the moon's gravity is weaker.

Mass is critical because it dictates the delicate equilibrium that defines a star, a balance between the inward pull of gravity and the outward push of light emanating from the star's core. Gravity is a direct result of mass, but the amount of energy generated in a star's core comes from mass as well. The more massive the star is, the more pressure there is in the star's center and the hotter it gets.

A star's radiance comes from nuclear fusion–specifically, squeezing hydrogen atoms together hard enough to create helium (though the actual process is a bit more complicated). This releases energy mostly in the form of gamma rays, which are absorbed by the surrounding material, heating it up. The rate of fusion depends on the star's core temperature, which depends on, yup, its mass. The rate depends very strongly on the core temperature, in fact: in a star like the sun, the fusion rate scales as the fourth power of the temperature, so a small change in temperature hugely affects how rapidly the core generates energy.

Higher-mass stars use a different fusion process that is *ridiculously* dependent on temperature; the fusion rate can scale with temperature to about the 20th power! This coupling is so strong that doubling the temperature in a massive star's core increases the energy generation rate by a factor of a *million*.

You might see now why stars can only get so big. If you pile on too much mass, the star's gravity strengthens, the pressure in the core rises, the temperature increases, and then the fusion rate skyrockets. If too much energy is dumped into the star's upper layers, they get so hot that they don't just expand; they also blast away material, thus losing mass. This forms a negative feedback loop that limits how massive a star can be. Also, stars in this frenzied state aren't terribly stable; the fusion rate can be tempestuous, and the star undergoes incredibly violent paroxysms.

The theoretical upper limit on stellar mass depends on other factors, too, but is probably around 300 times the sun's mass. Stars this bulky are incredibly rare, and only a few with more than 200 solar masses are known. The most massive star we know of is R136a1, a beast in the Large Magellanic Cloud, a satellite galaxy of the Milky Way. It's about 160,000 light-years away–which is fine by me! It blasts out seven million times as much energy as the sun, so keeping it in a different galaxy is a pretty good idea.

R136a1 is part of a stellar cluster called R136, which was thought to be a single star when it was first discovered. That was a problem because R136 is so luminous that it would need *thousands* of times the sun's mass to be so bright. Hubble Space Telescope observations, however, confirmed it was in fact a small cluster of stars. The brightest member, R136a1, is still a monster, though: it's estimated to have about 290 times the sun's mass—close to the theoretical limit. It's probably only about a million years old and will last roughly another two million before exploding as a supernova.

Because R136a1 is so near the top of the mass scale, we're unlikely to find another star that's so massive. But that hasn't always been the case.

Another factor in how massive a star can become is the abundance of heavy elements in its outer layers. Many of these are very good at absorbing the energy coming up from the star's interior, which makes the star hotter. If the star gets too hot, it blows away those outer layers. So, much like spicy seasoning, even a pinch of heavy elements can have an outsize effect.

In the very young universe, though, those elements didn't yet exist! Early on, matter in the cosmos was almost entirely hydrogen and helium (with only a soupçon of heavier elements such as lithium). Massive stars eventually churned out heavier elements later, first cooking these elements up in their cores via fusion and then making more when they inevitably exploded as supernovas, seeding gas clouds for the next generation of stars. Today those elements are relatively common, but that wasn't the case when the first generation of stars arose. Because of this, those earliest stars could become incredibly massive: some models show they could have had many thousands of times the sun's mass!

These genesis stars all lived and died early on in time line of the universe's existence, and their light would have traveled so far to reach us that, despite their immense luminosity, they would appear very faint if we were to spot them; no confirmed first-generation star has yet been seen (though there is at least one candidate).

Astronomers are vigorously searching for them, of course. Once confirmed, we'll have to greatly increase our estimate of how big a star could get—maybe not today but once upon a time. And when we do, we'll have learned another key factor in how stars are born, how they live and how they die—and how all that depends on what they're made of and when in the history of the cosmos we see them.

About the Author

Phil Plait is a professional astronomer and science communicator in Virginia. His column for Scientific American, *The Universe, covers all things space. He writes the* Bad Astronomy Newsletter. *Follow him online.*

Section 5: In a Galaxy Far, Far Away

The Scale of Space Will Break Your Brain

By Phil Plait

Space is big. That's why we call it space. But how big is "big"? That's relative. When an astronomer says something is nearby, they might mean it's a few million kilometers away (if they're talking asteroids) or a few tens of trillions (for stars) or a few tens of quintillions (for galaxies).

No matter the destination, it's a long walk. We make it easier on ourselves by using huge units to measure distance, such as a light-year, the distance traveled in a year by light–the fastest thing in the universe. A light-year is about 10 trillion kilometers (km). But that's still fairly abstract to the typical person reading casually about "nearby" exoplanets or "distant" galaxies. One way to better grasp this scale is to take it step by step. The moon is the closest astronomical object to us in the entire universe. On average across its orbital path, it's about 380,000 km from Earth. That's already a pretty long way; nearly 30 Earths could fit side by side over that distance! Or think of it this way: the Apollo astronauts, traveling faster than any human before them, took three days to reach the moon's vicinity.

The sun is about 400 times farther away from us than the moon is: 150 million km. How far is that? If you could pave a road between Earth and the sun, it would take you about 170 years to drive there at highway speeds. Better pack a lunch. A commercial jet would be better–it would take a mere 17 years.

When we work with objects inside the solar system, it's convenient to use the Earth-sun distance as a kind of cosmic meter stick. We call it the astronomical unit, or AU, and it is defined by the International Astronomical Union (the keeper of all astronomical numbers, names, and other such agreed-on conventions) as exactly 149,597,870.7 km. Mercury is about 0.4 AU from the sun and Venus about 0.7. Their distances from Earth depend on where all the planets are in their orbits and increase when respective planets are on opposite sides of the sun, so Venus will range from about 0.3 to 1.7 AU from Earth.

Neptune, the farthest major planet from the sun, is 4.5 billion km out, or 30 AU. Pluto's at roughly the same distance, and it's a long way from us. The New Horizons spacecraft took more than nine years to get there despite moving at speeds of more 50,000 km per hour.

These numbers are still difficult to grasp. When I traveled to schools to give demonstrations to kids about astronomy, one of my favorite props was the solar system rope: a hefty 15-meter cord that represented the average sun-to-Pluto distance. The students were given photos of planets, and we'd place them at the proper scaled distance from the sun. The inner four planets were so close together that the kids were practically on top of one another, but the outer planets were spread out a long way; we had to either find a long hallway or go outside for the demo.

That lesson proved so popular that I created a spreadsheet allowing anyone to calculate the solar system to scale. It's based on the size of the sun, so you can change it from the default of one meter to, say, the size of a grape and find out how big and how far-off the planets become. It's fun—and eye-opening.

But it's useful, too, to consider the separation between objects in terms of their size. For example, the sun is 1.4 million km wide. The nearest star system to the sun is Alpha Centauri, which is 41 trillion km away. If we divide the second number by the first, we find that Alpha Centauri is about 30 million "suns" away. Stars are very small compared with the distance between them, and that is one reason you really don't need to worry about one ever colliding with our sun!

That's also why we use light-years to measure these distances; it's a more palatable unit for dealing with interstellar journeys. Alpha Centauri is 4.3 light-years away. The Orion Nebula is about 1,250 light-years from the sun. The center of the Milky Way is

26,000 light-years away, and the galaxy itself is a flattish disk some 120,000 light-years across.

The nearest big galaxy to the Milky Way is Andromeda, which is 2.5 million light-years from us. That's an interesting number because it's "only" 20 times the size of the Milky Way. Most galaxies are pretty close in size.

Inside galaxies, stars collide extremely rarely because they're so far apart relative to their size. But galaxies are more crowded together in space, so it's not too big a surprise that galaxy collisions are not only common but ubiquitous. The Milky Way grew to its tremendous size by colliding and merging with other galaxies, and in fact every big galaxy has undergone multiple collisions.

The Milky Way and Andromeda are the two biggest galaxies in a clutch of about 100 galaxies that we call the Local Group. It's about 10 million light-years across. There are even bigger and more populous groups, called galaxy clusters. The nearest big one is the Virgo Cluster, with well over 1,000 galaxies in it, located about 50 million light-years from us. And smaller groups exist that are closer to us.

Galaxy clusters are held together by the gravity of their members and can be tens of millions of light-years wide. But we're not done! Clusters can clump up in the cosmos to form clusters of clusters, called superclusters. The Virgo Cluster and the Local Group are part of the Laniakea Supercluster, which may have more than 100,000 galaxies in it and stretches for 500 million light-years.

The universe is 13.8 billion years old, so you might think the most distant objects we can see are roughly that distance away in light-years. But the cosmos is expanding, and in the time it's taken for the light from distant objects to reach us, that expansion has swept them farther from us. Because of this movement, the observable universe is estimated to be more like 90 or so billion light-years across!

After all that, I'll let you in on a secret: even astronomers can't truly grasp these scales. We work with them, and we can do math and physics with them, but our ape brains still struggle to comprehend even the distance to the moon—and the universe is two million trillion times bigger than that.

So, yeah—space is big. And it's true that we are very, very small. These scales can seem crushing. But I'll leave you with this: although the cosmos is immense beyond what we can grasp, by using math and physics and our brain, we can actually understand it.

And that makes us pretty big, too.

About the Author

Phil Plait is a professional astronomer and science communicator in Virginia. His column for Scientific American, *The Universe, covers all things space. He writes the* Bad Astronomy Newsletter. *Follow him online.*

How Heavy is the Universe? Conflicting Answers Hint at New Physics

By Anil Ananthaswamy

Two entirely different ways of "weighing" the cosmos are producing disparate results. If more precise measurements fail to resolve the discrepancy, physicists may have to revise the standard model of cosmology, our best description of the universe.

"If this really is a glimpse of the standard model breaking down, that would be potentially revolutionary," says astronomer Hendrik Hildebrandt of the Ruhr University Bochum in Germany.

Similar concerns over the correctness of the standard model have been raised over the past few years by two independent calculations of the so-called Hubble constant, or the rate at which the universe is expanding today. Those two measurements also disagreed, creating what has been called the Hubble tension.

The new discrepancy–called the sigma-eight tension–involves measuring the density of matter in the universe and the degree to which it is clumped up, as opposed to being uniformly distributed. The result is encapsulated in a parameter called sigma-eight. To calculate sigma-eight, Hildebrandt and his colleagues turned to an effect called weak gravitational lensing, in which the light from distant galaxies is bent ever so slightly toward our telescopes because of the gravitational pull from matter that lies between the galaxies and Earth.

The resulting distortion is so small that it barely changes the shape of an individual galaxy. But if you take an average of the shapes of tens of thousands of galaxies in a patch of sky, a signal of weak lensing pops out. Presuming that galaxies should be randomly oriented with respect to Earth, their average shape should be nearly circular–without weak lensing, that is. But thanks to the mild distortions from this effect, the average shape instead veers toward the elliptical.

The astronomers used this signal to estimate the amount and distribution of intervening matter (both normal and dark varieties) along the lines of sight to various galaxy-rich regions across a large patch of the sky. In other words, they managed to measure matter's cosmic density.

But doing so precisely requires one more piece of information: the distance to each individual galaxy being studied. Normally, astronomers calculate the distance to another galaxy by finding its spectroscopic redshift—the amount by which the galaxy's light is shifted toward the longer wavelengths of the red side of the spectrum. The greater the redshift, the farther away the object.

Measuring individual spectroscopic redshifts, however, is extremely inefficient when dealing with millions of galaxies. So Hildebrandt's team turned to something called photometric redshift, which involves taking multiple images of the same patch of sky in different wavelengths, spanning the optical and near-infrared ranges. The researchers used those images to estimate the redshift of individual galaxies in each one. "They're not as good as the traditional spectroscopic redshift," Hildebrandt says. "But they're much more efficient in terms of telescope time."

For its entire analysis, the team used high-resolution images of hundreds of square degrees of the sky (the full moon is about half a degree across) in nine wavelength bands—four optical and five near-infrared. These observations of about 15 million galaxies were collected by the European Southern Observatory's Kilo-Degree Survey (KiDS) and VISTA Kilo-Degree Infrared Galaxy Survey (VIKING) using two small telescopes at the organization's Paranal Observatory in Chile.

The VIKING data bolstered the KiDS data set by providing multiple observations of the same region of the sky in near-infrared wavelengths. The greater the distances of a galaxy, the higher the speed at which it is receding from us. This causes more of a galaxy's light to be redshifted into the near-infrared range, so relying solely on optical observations is not enough. Infrared measurements capture a greater amount of the light from such galaxies, leading to better estimates of their photometric redshift.

To ensure that photometric redshifts are as accurate as possible, these observations were calibrated against spectroscopic redshift measurements of a few of the same galaxies made with the more massive eight-meter Very Large Telescope at Paranal and the 10-meter Keck telescopes on Mauna Kea in Hawaii.

Astrophysicist and Nobel laureate Adam Riess of Johns Hopkins University approves of the efforts of the KiDS researchers. "Their latest results use infrared data, which probably does a better job of tracing the mass of the lenses and getting reliable photometric redshifts," he says.

Using the combined data, covering about 350 square degrees of the sky, the astronomers estimated sigma-eight. The value they found conflicts with a sigma-eight figure calculated using the European Space Agency's Planck satellite's observations of the cosmic microwave background (CMB)–the earliest observable light in the universe, which was emitted about 380,000 years after the big bang. Planck mapped the variations in the temperature and polarization of the CMB from point to point in the sky. Cosmologists can employ the map to calculate the sigma-eight value for the early universe. Using the standard model of cosmology (which says that the cosmos is made of about 5 percent ordinary matter, 27 percent dark matter and 68 percent dark energy), they can then extrapolate across more than 13 billion years of cosmic evolution to estimate the present-day value for sigma-eight.

Herein lies the tension. Hildebrandt's weak-lensing study estimates sigma-eight to be about 0.74, whereas the Planck data provides a value of about 0.81."There is about a 1 percent chance or so that this [tension] is a statistical fluctuation," Hildebrandt says. Statistical fluctuations are random noise in data that can mimic actual signals and can disappear with more data. "This is not something to completely lose sleep over."

Not yet anyway. It is also possible a systematic error lurks in the calculations of one or both of the teams. After the researchers identify any such errors, the discrepancy could go away.

Or it may not do so, which has been the case with the Hubble tension. As astronomical measurements have become more precise, the statistical significance of the Hubble tension has only grown, inflicting sleepless nights on more than a few anxious theorists."Something very similar might happen with our sigma-eight discrepancy," Hildebrandt says. "We don't know."

Riess, who leads one of the teams estimating the Hubble constant using measurements of supernovae in the nearby universe, likens the sigma-eight tension to a "little brother or sister of the Hubble tension." That discrepancy is now considered statistically significant, with less than a one-in-3.5-million chance of being a fluke. The sigma-eight tension, with its one-in-100 chance of being a statistical aberration, is where the Hubble tension was a few years ago. "So [it is] less significant but worth keeping an eye on for a possible connection," Riess says.

If the sigma-eight tension ascends to the same level of statistical relevance as the Hubble tension, the pressure to reevaluate the standard model of cosmology could become too enormous to ignore. At that point, cosmologists may be forced to invoke new physics to bring the Planck estimates in line with the direct measurements of the parameters of the present-day universe. "That will be the exciting alternative," Hildebrandt says.

Potential "new physics" fixes to the standard model could involve changing the amount and nature of dark energy or dark matter–or both–as well as tweaks to how they interact with each other and with normal matter, among other more exotic modifications. "Some theoretical solutions to tinker with the cosmological model to fix the Hubble constant tension make this [sigma-eight tension] worse. Some make it better," Riess says.

Hildebrandt agrees that there is no obvious solution in sight. "If there was a compelling model, maybe people would jump on that bandwagon," he says. "But at the moment, I don't think there is. It's really on us observers to improve the significance [of the sigma-eight tension] or disprove it."

About the Author

Anil Ananthaswamy is author of The Edge of Physics *(Houghton Mifflin Harcourt, 2010),* The Man Who Wasn't There *(Dutton, 2015),* Through Two Doors at Once: The Elegant Experiment That Captures the Enigma of Our Quantum Reality *(Dutton, 2018), and* Why Machines Learn: The Elegant Math Behind Modern AI *(Dutton, 2024).*

How Many Holes Does the Universe Have?

By Manon Bischoff

Around 2,500 years ago humankind began to recognize that our planet is round—although a few "flat Earth" supporters still deny this today. The shape of our universe is not clear, however. Previous studies have suggested that the cosmos probably has a fairly simple shape, such as the three-dimensional equivalent of a spherical surface or a plane. But this view may be wrong, according to cosmologists from the Collaboration for Observations, Models and Predictions of Anomalies and Cosmic Topology (COMPACT). In a paper published in April 2024, they found that the shape of the universe could be significantly more complex than previously assumed.

Earth also appears flat at first glance. This is because its radius is so large that the surface's curvature is barely perceptible. To prove it's a sphere, you would just have to start walking. If you were to move straight ahead without ever turning—crossing over mountains and oceans—you would inevitably return to the start at some point.

Cosmologists collect similar clues to determine the shape of the universe. They could send a spaceship out to traverse the cosmos. Instead they peer into the night sky and examine traces of the oldest light that reaches us from the depths of the cosmos. This radiation was created around 300,000 years after the big bang. Although photons had existed even before that, matter was so densely packed into what was then a small universe that the light quanta had no chance of traveling freely. Eventually, however, the universe cooled down to such an extent that it became transparent. The photons were able to spread freely through space—and still do today.

Photons from this early time in the universe reach us as cosmic background radiation. Approximately the same pattern of old light comes from every corner of the universe. This radiation provides clues to the shape of the universe. If, for example, the curvature of the universe were to change at one point, the cosmic background radiation would not be as homogeneous as we observe it. Experts therefore assume that the universe is either curved in the same way everywhere—or is completely flat.

A Wealth of Possibilities

It is difficult to imagine the universe having no curvature or constant curvature. That's why it helps to use two-dimensional examples. In this analogy, to fit the homogeneous patterns of cosmic background radiation, the universe can be actually flat like a flat sheet of paper (no curvature), correspond to the three-dimensional counterpart of a spherical surface (positive curvature) or form a kind of three-dimensional saddle surface (negative curvature). In all three cases, the curvature is constant everywhere.

But this still does not reveal what the universe as a whole looks like. For example, space could be curved in the same way everywhere and still have a hole. The mathematical discipline of topology can be used to differentiate between such cases. Topologists classify geometric figures according to rough categories, such as the number of holes in them, in order to create a catalog of shapes. Cosmologists aim to assign one of these shapes to the universe.

As mathematicians have been able to prove, there are an infinite number of different categories (topologies) of curved three-dimensional surfaces. So if spacetime really is saddle-shaped or spherical, then there are theoretically any number of shapes that the universe can take on, each of which is very different from the other. Cosmological observations to date, however, point to a flat universe without curvature. If true, this insight narrows the search for the topology of the universe: as mathematician Grigori Perelman deduced in 2003, the catalog of flat three-dimensional surfaces is very small, with only 18 different categories.

One of 18 Shapes

The shape of the universe therefore presumably corresponds to one of these 18 shapes. One is the three-dimensional analog of a sheet of paper. Our cosmos could also have holes, however. Among the 18 topologies, the three-dimensional equivalent of a donut surface is a so-called torus.

Although a donut appears curved at first glance, it turns out that this shape is actually flat. This is because a donut shape can be created using a (very flexible) sheet of paper. To do this, you first stick the opposite long sides of the sheet together, creating an elongated tube. Then you bend the tube and bring the two openings together.

This construction has many advantages. For example, if you want to describe the movement of an ant on a donut, it is usually easier to imagine the rectangular sheet of paper. The insect walks around on the piece of paper and as soon as it crosses an edge, it reenters the opposite side of the sheet–as in the popular mobile game Snake from the 2000s. If the ant moves in a straight line, it will inevitably end up back at the start at some point.

You can create a three-dimensional torus in the same way by using a three-dimensional cuboid instead of a rectangular sheet of paper. In this case, you also deform it so that opposite sides of the cuboid are glued together.

A Donut Universe with Loops

If our universe were torus-shaped, this would have tangible consequences. If we were to shine a flashlight into the sky, for example, this light would theoretically reach us again at some point–just as the ant on the sheet of paper always returns to its starting point. Such loops exist in most of the 18 different topologies. These are trajectories that return to their starting point. At first glance, however, the loops do not seem to correspond to our observations. If light were to periodically pass through space, we would have to see several copies of the universe in the night sky.

Still, this fact does not exclude all topologies with loops. We could live in a universe so large that light has not yet had enough time to traverse it and return. Perhaps in several billion years, humans (or other beings) will have the pleasure of seeing a night sky that contains numerous images of the universe.

But even such huge loops would leave traces today. For example, the shape of the cosmos would have influenced how matter and light interacted with each other in the early universe. If the universe had holes—and therefore also loops—this fact should be reflected in the data of the cosmic background radiation.

Yet in searches from the 2000s and 2010s, experts found nothing. Most cosmologists have therefore assumed that the universe had a fairly simple structure. Research into the shape of the universe stalled—at least until COMPACT launched in 2022.

Significantly More Possibilities Than Expected

The COMPACT team compared the latest data on cosmological background radiation with various topologies of the universe—and came up with surprising results in its first publication. Among other things, the researchers discovered that previous work had ignored many variants of the individual topologies. In other words, researchers may have previously missed other forms that could describe our cosmos. The collaboration was also able to show that the missing evidence for loops in the cosmic background radiation is far less restrictive than previously assumed. In addition to loops, there could be other traces in the cosmic background radiation that point to complicated topologies. Future work will explore what exactly these shapes could be.

The researchers backed up their arguments using three concrete example topologies of flat space: an ordinary torus and two variations of it in which the faces of the cuboid are twisted before being glued together. All three have holes. For the ordinary torus, COMPACT confirmed earlier conclusions: if our universe is torus-shaped, the loops must be so large that light has not yet been able to reach us. But the surprise was that this same idea may not apply to the modified shapes. The collaboration's calculations show that loops of these shapes could also be significantly shorter than what was assumed from the previous data. Because of the many twists, the universe could contain copies of itself that might look different from the original, making them less easy to spot in maps of the cosmic microwave background.

Taken together, the COMPACT team's findings show that the universe could look far more complicated than previously assumed. And that would have far-reaching consequences. The shape of our cosmos is not just an academic question. The topology of spacetime was presumably determined by the quantum processes that took place shortly after the big bang. If we knew more about the shape of the universe, we could—potentially—learn more about the complex processes that took place at its beginning.

About the Author

Manon Bischoff is a theoretical physicist and an editor at Spektrum der Wissenschaft, *the German-language sister publication of* Scientific American.

Faster-Than-Light Galaxies Are a Fact of Life in Our Expanding Universe

By Phil Plait

If there is an absolute law in the universe, it's that nothing can travel faster than the speed of light.

For science-fiction enthusiasts, that's a bit depressing. Space is *big*, and while the speed of light is incredibly fast to us humans, on interstellar scales it's glacially slow. Even at a photon's speed of about 300,000 kilometers per second, it's a journey of more than four years to reach just the closest star to the sun.

But we have to be careful how we state this universal law. To be more specific, nothing can move faster than the speed of light *through* space. That may seem like a nitpick, but it turns out to have literally cosmic importance.

To see why, we have to look at the behavior of the universe itself. One of the most important things the universe does is *expand*. It's getting bigger every day. The foundational observations for this, which were made more than a century ago, showed that distant galaxies appeared to be receding from us—not only that, but ones farther away were moving faster.

That's what an explosion does: at some time after the bang, the fastest-moving material will be farthest away. This is where the idea of the big bang model for the origin of the universe comes from.

The cosmic expansion can be measured as a rate, meaning at a given distance from us, a galaxy will be moving away from us at given speed. At a different distance, a galaxy will be moving at a different speed. We measure this as a rate of expansion called the Hubble constant. Our best measurements of this give a value of about 70 kilometers per second per megaparsec. In other words, a galaxy one megaparsec from us (about 3.26 million light-years) will be receding at 70 km/sec. A galaxy two megaparsecs away will be moving twice as fast, or at 140 km/sec, and so on.

Extrapolating this, though, runs us into trouble: it's not hard to see that at some distance from us, the recession speed will equal the speed of light. If you run the numbers, just using the speed of light divided by the Hubble constant, you find that distance is about 14 billion light-years. That distance is called the Hubble sphere, and anything farther away than that would be—from our perspective—moving faster than light.

Here's where things get weird. ("Oh yes, *here* is where that happens," I expect you're thinking.) The universe is actually quite a bit bigger than that. We know the cosmos was born about 13.8 billion years ago. By some few hundreds of millions of years later, galaxies had formed. When we see the light from a distant galaxy, it's taken, say, 12 billion years to reach us, but over that time, the universe has expanded. So the light has actually had to travel much farther than 12 billion light-years to get to us. By the time the light reaches us, that galaxy is more like 23 billion light-years away.

That means there are galaxies outside our Hubble sphere, and they are moving away from us faster than the speed of light! How is that possible?

And now we come back to choosing our words carefully. Yes, nothing can move through space faster than light. But those galaxies aren't moving through space. They're moving *with* it.

Because—to belabor this point—space itself is expanding, and that changes everything. The ultimate speed limit only matters for material objects, but space isn't included in that definition. It can expand at whatever rate it wants, and that means at some distance from us it is expanding faster than light. Galaxies, embedded in the fabric of space, are swept along with it, so past some threshold—in this case, the boundary of the Hubble sphere—they move away from us at superluminal speeds.

An imperfect analogy: Imagine a boat on the ocean that can move across the water at 20 km/hour. If the boat is headed away from you, that's how fast you'll see it moving. But now imagine the boat's in a current moving at 30 km/hour away from you. You'd now measure the boat moving at 50 km/hour, even though the speed of the boat relative to the water is only 20. To be clear, this is only an analogy and shouldn't be taken too far. But it helps to picture how this works.

So galaxies can move away from us faster than light. But can we see them?

Naively you'd think the answer is no because space is expanding too rapidly for light to catch up to us. But that's not actually the case. Imagine a galaxy just outside our Hubble sphere. We see it moving away at just faster than light. But from its point of view, the light it emits can easily reach the edge of our Hubble sphere after some time because that edge is not as far from that galaxy. And once that light passes over that distance, it can, by definition, reach us! This means we can in fact see galaxies outside that distance, even though those galaxies are receding faster than light. Incidentally, this also means that from the perspective of galaxies just outside our own Hubble sphere, the Milky Way is moving away from them at superluminal speed. That's right: from a certain cosmic point of view, you're breaking a universal speed limit right now, even if you're sitting motionless in a chair.

Does your head hurt yet? Yeah, I get it. But in fact I'm being quite gentle and hand-wavy about this because it's all so extremely complex. To truly understand, you have to invoke Einstein's general theory of relativity, which complicates matters greatly. Relativistic physics describes all this very well, but translating it into words is difficult. It's like trying to describe a symphony with words alone; you can talk about its volume and pitch, but without hearing the music, those words can't possibly truly describe it.

It amazes me that so many people not only understand the implications of general relativity but use that physics in their day-to-day life trying to understand the universe's behavior—a study called cosmology. And it's more wondrous that someone came up with this idea in the first place. Einstein was pretty smart, it turns out.

But it also took a huge number of astronomers from all over the world working over the past century to get us to where we are now in that cosmic exploration. And we're still very far from understanding it all. There's still so much left to learn, and—in an expanding universe—we may never reach its limit.

About the Author

Phil Plait is a professional astronomer and science communicator in Virginia. His column for Scientific American, *The Universe, covers all things space. He writes the* Bad Astronomy Newsletter. *Follow him online.*

What's the Most Distant Galaxy? And Why Does It Matter?

By Phil Plait

As a science communicator, I don't think a week goes by without a press release hitting my inbox informing me of astronomers finding some new record-breaking object.

Sometimes it's the smallest planet yet discovered or the most iron-deficient star. But a very common claim is a distance record: the farthest galaxy from Earth ever seen, for example.

When it comes to these sorts of record breakers, I have complicated feelings, built over decades of writing about them. Such announcements must be parsed carefully because sometimes they're not that big of a deal—but sometimes they signal a sea change in what we can do or understand.

Distance records are an excellent proxy for the state of the art in astronomy. Finding extremely faraway galaxies is hard. In general, objects get smaller and fainter with distance (although bizarre exceptions do sometimes apply), so huge telescopes are needed to spot them at all.

Then comes the difficulty of actually determining their distance. We can't do this directly; it's not like we can hop onboard the starship *Enterprise* and keep our eyes on the odometer as we warp our way there. So we gauge distances in other ways.

The most well established method is to observe redshift: The universe is expanding, and as it does so, space sweeps galaxies along with it. Light leaving a distant galaxy loses energy as it fights that expansion, so by the time it reaches us, its wavelength is stretched, which is what astronomers call a redshift. For historical (and mathematical) reasons, we say that a photon with its wavelength stretched out by a factor of two has a redshift of one; if the wavelength is three times longer, the redshift is two, and so on. Because the velocity at which a galaxy recedes from us is related to its distance, finding the redshift of a galaxy can be used to measure that distance.

That's not an easy task either because converting redshift to distance involves understanding some rather arcane features of the universe–such as how much normal matter, dark matter and dark energy it contains, to name only a few. But we have accurate enough numbers for those parameters to get a decent grasp on distances.

And this is where "record-breaking" really comes in. I'll sometimes see a paper or announcement about a new galaxy that breaks the previous record–but it'll have a redshift of, say, 7.34, when the previous record was 7.33. That difference is pretty small! And depending on your preferred values for cosmic parameters, the difference might add up to just a million light-years. In our example of an object at a redshift of 7.34, we're talking distances of around 13 billion light-years, so the record-breaker is not exactly lapping the other galaxy. Also, it's not really telling us too much about the nature of the cosmos to simply find a galaxy that ekes out a win over another by a nose (or, I suppose, a spiral arm).

On the other hand, there are times such records do tell us something important.

When I was working on the Hubble Space Telescope in the late 1990s, it was becoming common to find objects with a redshift of around 6.0 because the observatory was designed, in part, to be able to see extremely distant galaxies. Some objects were found that might be even more distant, but many were difficult to confirm. Over time, astronomers using Hubble and other telescopes managed to glimpse galaxies even farther away using clever techniques such as fortuitous gravitational lensing.

Then, in 2021, our capabilities took a giant leap with the launch of the James Webb Space Telescope. Its infrared eye is more sensitive to extremely redshifted objects, and its huge 6.5-meter mirror outmatches Hubble's smaller optics for gathering photons. Soon papers were published with claims of galaxies at redshifts of 10, 11 and even higher–and while many of those preliminary measurements wound up being spurious, several were ultimately confirmed out to redshifts greater than 14. This is one of those times that a record breaker is important: it's telling us that we have a new way to observe the cosmos, which usually results in a new era of astronomical discovery.

For what it's worth, at the time of this writing the current record holder is a very luminous red blob of a galaxy called MoM-z14 at a redshift of 14.44. But by the time you read this, who knows?

Those records have significant scientific meaning as well. For example, light travels very rapidly but not infinitely so. It takes billions of years for the light from these vastly removed galaxies to reach us, which means that the farther away they are, the earlier in the time line of the cosmos we see them. Any new record means we've added information about our knowledge of the early universe, and sometimes it even means we're seeing the universe in a different stage of its development.

For example, when the cosmos was very young, it was opaque. But then, at some point, stars and supermassive black holes formed, spewing out energy and making it transparent. As we discover galaxies from that period, we can learn about the environment of space at that time, just a few hundred million years after the universe formed.

We also learn about galaxies themselves. Why do they shine so brightly at that age? They have supermassive black holes prodigiously feeding on infalling matter, but how did those black holes grow so huge so rapidly? The more distant a galaxy we find, the more data we have to unravel those mysteries.

Also, that database of distant objects can be used to learn about them in general. We might find that most distant galaxies have some average luminosity, with a few topping out a bit above that and none being brighter. That would tell us about the physics of how galaxies form, how they grow and how they emit light. If there is a single most brilliant distant galaxy, that could put firm limits on how they behave.

And there's another record that will be difficult to break or even verify. When we look back far enough, we won't see any more galaxies at all. Why not? Because they wouldn't have formed yet! It took a few hundred million years for galaxies to collect themselves, with dark matter serving as gravitational scaffolding, allowing normal matter to gather and condense, collecting in colossal quantities that would eventually form nebulas, stars and planets. If we can see far enough into the distant cosmos, far enough into the past, we'll be peering back in time to before those structures even existed.

To be fair, we already have done this; microwave telescopes have detected the fireball of the big bang, the leftover light from the original expansion of the universe that fills the sky as a gently glowing long-wavelength background (as distance records go, it's at a redshift of about 1,000!). But there's a several-hundred-million-year gap between that moment and the time at which galaxies first started popping up, and we know very little about it. Every record breaker we find squeezes that boundary a little tighter.

The universe is lovely, dark and deep, but with our powerful telescopes and clever brains, we keep pushing farther into it. For that, I welcome every new record that falls. At this point in our search, each one that's broken is a footstep into new astronomical territory.

About the Author

Phil Plait is a professional astronomer and science communicator in Virginia. His column for Scientific American, *The Universe, covers all things space. He writes the* Bad Astronomy Newsletter. *Follow him online.*

JWST Spots Most Distant Galaxy Ever, Pushing the Limits of the Observable Universe

By Jackie Flynn Mogensen

In a galaxy far, far away, there lie clues to the cosmic dawn—the first few hundreds of millions of years in our 13.8-billion-year-old universe's early history. On Wednesday astronomers on announced that a bright galaxy called MoM-z14 that was found using NASA's James Webb Space Telescope (JWST) is the farthest yet detected, existing just 280 million years after the big bang.

"With Webb, we are able to see farther than humans ever have before, and it looks nothing like what we predicted, which is both challenging and exciting," said Rohan Naidu, an astronomer at the Massachusetts Institute of Technology and the lead author of a preprint paper detailing MoM-z14's discovery that will soon be published in the overlay journal *Open Journal of Astrophysics*, in a statement in NASA's announcement.

The galaxy, the light of which has taken more than 13 billion years to reach our telescopes, is brighter, denser and more chemically rich than astronomers had expected, according to NASA.

To pinpoint galaxies like MoM-z14, astronomers use redshift. Essentially, this is the measure of how stretched the light coming from an object is as a result of that object moving away from our perspective as the universe expands. The higher the redshift, the farther the object is. In MoM-z14's case, it has a redshift of 14.4—a record, *Scientific American* columnist Phil Plait noted late last year.

But records are made to be broken. And NASA said it fully expects this new JWST achievement to be surpassed in the not-too-distant future as its observations improve.

Regardless, MoM-z14 could offer new clues to the early universe, including, for instance, why it and other early galaxies are so bright.

"It's an incredibly exciting time, with Webb revealing the early universe like never before," said Yijia Li, a Pennsylvania State University graduate student, who also contributed to the research, in the same statement, "and showing us how much there still is to discover."

About the Author

Jackie Flynn Mogensen is a breaking news reporter at Scientific American. *Before joining* SciAm, *she was a science reporter at* Mother Jones, *where she received a National Academies Eric and Wendy Schmidt Award for Excellence in Science Communications in 2024. Mogensen holds a master's degree in environmental communication and a bachelor's degree in earth sciences from Stanford University. She is based in New York City.*

When a Galaxy Erupts, What We See Depends on How We See It

By Phil Plait

Standing on Earth and gazing out into the night sky, you'd think our Milky Way galaxy is relatively calm. Oh sure, there's the occasional supernova and a bit of unrest as huge gas clouds collide and start to form stars. But as a whole, the vast cosmic neighborhood in which we live feels stately. Most nearby galaxies we can see look that way as well, just quietly going about their cosmic business. Tranquil.

But that's not the case for all galaxies. Centaurus A is an overly enthusiastic oddball approximately 13 million light-years from Earth. It appears to be an elliptical galaxy shaped like a roundish cotton ball but with a striking dark lane across its middle. In the 1940s astronomers discovered it was inexplicably blasting out radio waves from its core–and subsequent studies across the ensuing decades showed that its center was also emitting high-energy x-rays and even gamma rays. Clearly Centaurus A has a lot more going on than you'd suspect at first glance. Observers eventually found many other similar objects, which were collectively given the catchall name Seyfert galaxies (after American astronomer Carl Seyfert, who discovered several of them).

Then, in the 1960s, things got weirder. Astronomers started discovering objects that emitted powerful radio waves but, unlike most Seyfert galaxies, were very faint in visible light. Many of those newfound objects were incredibly far away and therefore extremely luminous, but looked so much like stars that they were dubbed quasi-stellar radio sources, or quasars for short. Deep images taken with large telescopes revealed each observed quasar to be an extraordinarily bright central point of light drastically outshining a much fainter surrounding galaxy.

As astronomers were wrapping their heads around the mysteries of quasars, yet another galaxy exhibiting a different sort of strange behavior drew their attention: BL Lacertae (or BL Lac for short). At nearly a billion light-years away, it too is a ridiculously luminous powerhouse, but amazingly it also changes its brightness dramatically over short periods of time, sometimes just a few hours. It was the first of a class of galaxies given the name blazars, a clever triple portmanteau of BL Lac, blazing and quasar. Like Seyferts and quasars, the majority of their light comes from their very centers. Together all three flavors are lumped into a broad category called active galactic nuclei, or AGN for short.

It didn't take astronomers long to figure out what could possibly power such fierce and concentrated energy emission: a supermassive black hole gobbling down lots of matter. Still, if this is the engine behind all AGN, why do quasars, Seyferts and blazars all appear so different from each other?

In the 1990s astronomers came up with a brilliant idea to unify these disparate characteristics. While there is some actual physical diversity among these galaxies, the majority of their differing properties could be explained more by how we see them.

I mean this literally: the angle at which we view their centers greatly affects the resulting light we see. Understanding why that is essentially boils down to what exactly is happening near that central supermassive black hole.

Far out from the black hole, thousands to tens of thousands of light-years away, is a relatively normal galaxy not too different from the Milky Way. But closer in, where the gravity of the black hole holds sway, things are very different.

Immediately surrounding the monster black hole is a flat disk of matter (called an accretion disk) upon which it feeds. This accretion disk can stretch for several trillion kilometers, a decent fraction of a light-year, and it's hot. The material very close to the black hole is orbiting at speeds approaching that of light, but farther out, the material is moving much more slowly. This creates immense friction in the disk that can heat matter up to millions of degrees. At this temperature and density, the material is incredibly bright and can easily outshine all of the galaxy's stars.

The disk has an intense magnetic field embedded in it. As matter in the disk approaches the black hole and increases its orbital speed, the embedded magnetic field can coil up like thread around a spool. This further strengthens the magnetic field, which can become so powerful (coupled with a bizarre effect called frame dragging in which the black hole's spin itself drags the fabric of spacetime around it) that material is expelled from the disk and blasted away in a pair of beams called jets. These jets are highly focused and stupendously powerful, and they can create immense internal shock waves that in turn unleash torrents of gamma rays—the highest-energy form of light in the cosmos. The jets can flow for hundreds of thousands of light-years in some cases, extending well outside the galaxy itself.

Crucially, farther out from the accretion disk and jets, on a scale of dozens to hundreds of light-years across in some cases, there is a dust torus—a doughnut-shaped cloud of tiny grains of rock and carbonaceous material. This stuff is dense and opaque to visible light, and if thick enough, it can block higher-energy forms of radiation as well.

In the unified model of AGN, the angle at which we see these structures explains almost everything we see. If the jets are pointed more or less toward Earth, we see light from across the electromagnetic spectrum, from gamma rays down to radio waves. Those are the blazars. If we see an AGN at a slightly lower angle, then the jet is aimed away, and the beamlike gamma-ray emissions miss us, but we can still detect high-energy x-rays; these are the quasars.

At lower angles still, the dust torus starts to the block the highest-energy light from reaching us. In these cases, much of an AGN's emission is so dimmed that its surrounding galaxy is more readily visible. These are the Seyferts, and they tend to be bright in radio waves and infrared because their dust is warmed by the hellish brew closer in to the center, producing infrared thermal radiation.

The situation is a bit like the parable of the blind men and the elephant: what you think you see depends on which part you're seeing, and it's only when you put the pieces together that the true picture emerges. For active galaxies, the unified model does a good job at explaining the broad differences between the classes of galaxies observed.

To be honest, though, the unified model doesn't explain everything, and it can struggle to reproduce many details that we see. But that's not surprising: any model is going to be incomplete and isn't going to explain every single thing found in every observation. The idea is to have a general sense of the processes and structures involved to explain a majority of what's seen. Then extensions to the model can be introduced to explain the outliers.

And what of our own Milky Way? We have a supermassive black hole at the heart of our home galaxy, but like many of our galactic neighbors, it's quiescent, meaning it's not currently feasting on matter. The key word there is "currently": It's likely that in the distant past the Milky Way's central black hole has episodically glutted itself on matter, too, each time erupting as an AGN. And because we tend to see AGN at large distances–when the universe was younger–this implies that most large galaxies have a similarly tempestuous youth. But happily, for now, we are at peace.

About the Author

Phil Plait is a professional astronomer and science communicator in Virginia. His column for Scientific American, *The Universe, covers all things space. He writes the* Bad Astronomy Newsletter. *Follow him online.*

Our Milky Way's Warped Disk Keeps Getting Weirder

By Phil Plait

Well, it's confession time: I've been lying to you.

I've said on many occasions in this column that our Milky Way galaxy has a flat disk. But it's not really flat—not according to any reasonable definition of the term, at least.

Now, in my defense, I wasn't exactly prevaricating; I was *simplifying*. That's a perfectly acceptable and even advantageous thing to do in science. When you're trying to understand or explain some complex thing, it helps to make it as simple as possible so that the math and physics are easier to crack. It's like assuming, at first, that Earth is a perfect sphere or that the sun contains all the mass in the solar system. Once you work out the basic equations that describe your simplified model, you can gradually add complexity back in—but in a way that makes the problem tractable.

To be fair, when you look at the glow of the Milky Way from a dark site, it does look flat—flat-ish. And lots of similar galaxies and their disks also appear flat.

But many of them, maybe even most of them, aren't. They're wiggly and wavy and bendy. Our galaxy is part of this warped group.

First, a quick overview: The Milky Way is classified as a disk galaxy, with a broad, circular collection of stars, gas and dust about 120,000 light-years across. It's a few thousand light-years thick, so "flat" is at least a decent adjective to use for it. In its center is a bulge of stars, and the entire thing is surrounded by a vast halo of stars and dark matter about a million light-years wide.

That last bit is important. Hang on a minute, and I'll explain why.

We've known for some time that out toward its edges, the disk of the Milky Way is warped—flared up on one side and down on the other rather like the brim of a fedora. Research published in the journal Science in 2019, however, refined this idea considerably.

The team of astronomers behind that paper used data from Gaia, a now retired European Space Agency mission that mapped the positions, motions and distances of more than a billion stars. They specifically looked at Gaia's observations of some 2,400 Cepheid variables—special kinds of stars that pulsate, changing in brightness. The time it takes for a Cepheid's brightness to change is related to its luminosity, the amount of energy it gives off. By comparing a Cepheid's intrinsic luminosity with how bright the star appears in our sky, we can calculate its distance.

By mapping so many Cepheids in the galactic plane, the scientists were able to trace the overall shape of the Milky Way's disk, and they found that the warping really stands out. Our galaxy looks a bit like a vinyl LP that's been out in the sun too long (kids, ask your grandparents).

What causes such warping? It's possible for a collision with a smaller galaxy to gravitationally affect the stars in a disk, similar to the way a rock tossed into a pond creates spreading ripples. But astronomers who presented their research in *Nature Astronomy* in 2023 had a very different idea for what's been tugging on our galaxy's brim: dark matter.

As I mentioned earlier, the galaxy is embedded in a halo of stars and dark matter. About a year before publishing their paper, some of the members of this team, along with other astronomers, found that the stellar halo was not spherical, as previously assumed, but instead was elongated and squished a little like a slightly flattened American football. It was also tilted with respect to the plane of the galaxy.

They posited that the more diffuse and nigh-invisible dark matter halo might have the same shape as the stellar halo. By modeling the effects that the much more massive dark matter halo would have if it were structured and oriented in a similar way, they found that this formation naturally created a gravitational field that tugged on the disk, which would explain not just the shape and size of the warp but also its orientation in the disk. Although this isn't necessarily case closed, they do make a pretty solid argument.

But that's not the only way our galaxy's disk is off-kilter. New research shows it's also corrugated.

Last year another group of scientists used Gaia data to look at 17,000 young stars–which tend to form right in the middle of the galaxy's disk–and 3,400 Cepheid variables in a region of the Milky Way tens of thousands of light-years across. They found that in the main disk and well into the warped outer parts, there is an up-and-down wave that strongly resembles the corrugation pattern in thick cardboard.

It's similar to the "wave" fans do at sports games, where they stand up and sit back down in a swell that moves around the stadium. In the Milky Way's case, the stars in the galaxy move up and down relative to the plane of the disk. Because so many of the stars the researchers measured are young, the scientists think the gas in the galaxy–which forms stars–moves up and down as well. So whatever this pattern is, it's intrinsic to the structure of the disk.

The cause of this wave isn't known, but the most likely culprit is, this time, a collision with a smaller galaxy. One potential, even probable, guilty party is the Sagittarius Dwarf Spheroidal galaxy, a small object with a tiny fraction of the Milky Way's mass. It orbits our galaxy in a nearly vertical loop, diving through the disk as it goes. In 2018 astronomers published a paper in *Nature* reporting that they had found–again, using Gaia data–wavelike motions in six million stars within approximately 10,000 light-years of the sun, similar to the waves found in the outer disk. They suggest that the Sagittarius galaxy might have created these structures the last time it passed through the disk, several hundred million years ago.

The sun also displays this motion; careful measurements show it has a vertical velocity as it orbits the galactic center. Our solar system bobs up and down with it. Every so often it moves through the disk, but after it reaches some distance from it, the gravity of the disk pulls it back, and the cycle starts again. This element of our star's motion may be a part of that greater wave.

So, as you can see, I wasn't really lying before about our flat disk. I was simply eliding over details that aren't necessary in a discussion of the overall structure of the galaxy. Yet it's certainly worth looking at these extra effects—they tell us about the history of our Milky Way and can even reveal how the sun plays its part as well.

About the Author

Phil Plait is a professional astronomer and science communicator in Virginia. His column for Scientific American, *The Universe, covers all things space. He writes the* Bad Astronomy Newsletter. *Follow him online.*

JWST Unveils Most Intricate Map Yet of Cosmic Dark Matter

By Joseph Howlett

It's an open secret in astronomy that, practically wherever the James Webb Space Telescope (JWST) looks in the sky, a vast, clump-filled mist fills its view. But luckily for everyone marveling at JWST's crisp snapshots of faraway galaxies, this dense haze is totally invisible.

That lightless, see-through murk is dark matter. Think of dark matter as scaffolding for all the luminous, normal stuff out there—with the former outweighing the latter five times over—like a gravitational glue that holds everything else together. But scientists have no idea what this "glue" is made of and have yet to detect it directly; they have only inferred its presence through subtle but unmistakable clues. For something so integral to all we see, it's astonishingly hidden from our cosmic view.

Now astronomers have traced dark matter's ghostly contours in the foreground of one of JWST's deep-sky images. They've turned a survey of the Cosmic Evolution Survey (COSMOS) field—one of the sky's best-studied patches—into the most finely detailed dark matter map in existence. With it, they hope to learn more about how galaxies depend on its presence. A study reporting the results appears today in *Nature Astronomy*.

"We can see the influence of gravity on galaxy formation," says Diana Scognamiglio, a postdoctoral fellow at NASA's Jet Propulsion Laboratory, who co-led the study. "It's a way to trace, really, the backbone of the universe."

Gaze upon any JWST image of some faraway galaxy. What you really see is where each ray of light hit JWST's optics during observations. The image essentially traces each ray back to its source within a targeted galaxy.

But that ray's journey from the galaxy to JWST isn't really a straight line. On its voyage through intergalactic space, that light traverses countless clumps of dark matter. Each clump slightly warps the spacetime around it, altering the light ray's path much like a glass lens.

That warping distorts the image in the same way that wearing someone else's glasses blurs your sight. For JWST's images, this effect is imperceptible to the eye, which is why it's called "weak gravitational lensing." But the images encode all the dark matter between the far-off object and the telescope.

No one knew how to decode this warping, however, until around the start of the third millennium. "People were saying that there's absolutely no way you can measure a 1 percent distortion with everything else going on," says Catherine Heymans, a professor of astrophysics at the University of Edinburgh and Scotland's astronomer royal. Heymans and her peers proved them wrong, launching the field of "weak lensing" that has since shed more light on dark matter.

Heymans helped build the first dark matter map of the COSMOS field using JWST's predecessor, the Hubble Space Telescope. "It was a really pioneering work," Scognamiglio says.

Two decades later Scognamiglio's team of cosmic cartographers has updated that map using the heaps more galaxies JWST's images contain. "It's super exciting just because of the sheer number of galaxies and that they can use," says Zoltan Haiman, an astrophysicist at Columbia University. The new map spans an area on the sky only twice as big as the full moon—a quarter of the original's size—but it's far more detailed, pinpointing blobs of dark matter that are too small for Hubble to discern.

And JWST's larger, more sensitive optics can collect light from farther out in the universe—and thus further back in cosmic time. So it can see weak lensing caused by dark matter clumps from 10 billion or 11 billion years ago, when the universe was most prodigiously forming stars and galaxies. Studying these clumps—which likely host clusters of adolescent galaxies–is a rare chance to learn more about what dark matter's role was in that epoch, called "cosmic noon," and how the universe has evolved ever since. Next the team wants to infer the various distances of the structures that the researchers have glimpsed and to use them to make the map more dynamic and three-dimensional.

For now, the map as is puts one of the universe's most elusive sculptors starkly in view. "Before we only had dark matter simulations, and I always wanted to be able to see it," Heyman says. "What I love about weak lensing is: it allows us to see the invisible."

In the coming years, astronomers' dark matter maps will be massively extended–though with less fine-grained detail. Weak lensing is part of the stated mission of newer space telescopes such as the European Space Agency's Euclid, already in orbit, and NASA's Nancy Grace Roman Space Telescope, scheduled for launch this year. Ground-based projects such as the Dark Energy Survey, which released a new trove of data last week, and the Vera C. Rubin Observatory also use weak lensing to study the universe's expansion.

A generation after the trailblazing Hubble dark matter map, Scognamiglio is proud to help extend its legacy. "I like this continuity," she says. "I hope that, 20 years from now, my student will be able to make an even better map."

About the Author

Joseph Howlett is a staff reporter at Scientific American *covering physics, math, astronomy and more. He was previously a math staff writer at* Quanta Magazine, *and holds a Ph.D. in particle physics from Columbia University.*

JWST's Puzzling Early Galaxies Bend Astrophysics

By Jonathan O'Callaghan

Ever since it opened its giant infrared eye on the cosmos after its December 2021 launch, the James Webb Space Telescope (JWST) has been finding an overabundance of bright galaxies that stretch back to the very early universe. Their brightness—a proxy for their number of stars and hence their mass—is deeply puzzling because galaxies shouldn't have had enough time to become so bulky in such early cosmic epochs. Imagine visiting a foreign land and finding that many of the toddlers there weigh as much as teenagers. You might have questions, too: Are the children so large because of something in the water, or might it instead be that your grasp of human growth is fundamentally flawed? Theorists who pondered JWST's big, bright early galaxies felt much the same: Was something fundamental amiss in our understanding of cosmology? Namely, was our knowledge of the expansion of the universe after the big bang simply wrong?

The answer, it appears, need not be quite so dramatic. Several studies investigating some of these early galaxies now point toward an astrophysical explanation for the unexpected girth—such as earlier-forming black holes or bursts of star formation—rather than some physics-shattering result. "Most people would put their money on the astrophysical explanation right now," says Mike Boylan-Kolchin, a cosmologist at the University of Texas at Austin. "I'd count myself in that category as well."

Before JWST's debut, its predecessor, the Hubble Space Telescope, held the record for the earliest galaxy ever found. We can see that object, called GN-z11, as it was about 13.4 billion years ago, around 400 million years after the big bang. Once JWST turned its gaze on the universe, however, it repeatedly smashed Hubble's record. Scientists are now studying galaxies stretching back to at least 320 million years after the big bang. And later this year fresh data releases from ongoing JWST galaxy surveys should push this record back even further.

The oldest galaxies JWST found were brighter and more active than expected, with star-formation rates comparable to the one-star-per-year rate of the Milky Way today. But they were squeezed into much more compact regions around one one-thousandth the size of our galaxy. And as JWST peered deep into the early universe, it also examined a more recent swath of cosmic history, up to about 750 million years after the big bang. The older galaxies it found there were still quite young and strange: they were about one-thirtieth the size of the Milky Way (much bigger than expected) and had star-formation rates that must have been 1,000 times higher than our galaxy's. Scientists called these relatively older systems ultramassive galaxies and kept scratching their heads: neither set of galaxies could be wholly explained by current models.

In the journal *Physical Review Letters*, Nashwan Sabti of Johns Hopkins University and his colleagues recently proposed an explanation for JWST's ultramassive galaxies. They used existing data from Hubble to examine hundreds of galaxies in ultraviolet light in the same epoch of the universe as these galaxies, about 450 million to 750 million years after the big bang. Unlike JWST, which observes primarily in infrared, Hubble is sensitive to the UV end of the electromagnetic spectrum, where young massive stars blaze brightest. Hubble's UV observations allowed the researchers to better gauge the rates of star formation in the mysterious ultramassive galaxies. "So we have the star-formation rate–the change in stellar mass over time–versus the stellar mass itself from JWST," Sabti says.

By comparing those two pieces of information, Sabti and his colleagues found that the galaxies could be explained within the confines of our cosmological model of the universe, the Lambda Cold Dark Matter (Lambda-CDM) model. It best replicates the observed patterns and properties of galaxies and other large cosmic structures. No esoteric physics were required. In fact, any such tweaks would put the Hubble observations at odds with JWST; the galaxies were growing exactly as expected in accordance with Lambda-CDM's predictions. "We showed that Hubble really doesn't give you much wiggle room to play around with cosmology," Sabti says. "That means the source [of the ultramassive galaxies] is very likely astrophysics."

Boylan-Kolchin says the paper makes a "great point" in comparing Hubble and JWST data from this period of the universe. He isn't completely convinced just yet, however. "I don't think the case is airtight that it has to be an astrophysical explanation," he says. "The loophole is that you're not necessarily observing the same galaxies with JWST and Hubble. Galaxies can be luminous [in infrared] for JWST but invisible for Hubble. If the most massive ones happen to be in that [infrared] regime, then maybe Hubble wouldn't be seeing them."

Sabti's paper is not the only recent work that points toward an astrophysical explanation for JWST's peculiar galaxies, however. Earlier this year in the *Astrophysical Journal Letters*, Joseph Silk of Johns Hopkins and Sorbonne University in Paris and his colleagues looked at the earliest galaxies seen by JWST, which predate GN-z11. The researchers wrote that there might be a way to grow the galaxies more quickly in the universe if black holes formed earlier than the galaxies, within the first 50 million years after the big bang. That could explain why star-formation rates in the early universe were so high: the black holes could have powered the galaxies earlier than expected and crushed clouds of dust and gas into stars more quickly. The mechanism involves reasonably well-understood astrophysical processes called feedback and outflow.

"There are far more black holes than we expected" in JWST's observations, Silk says, "and the galaxies they're in are very compact," barely 300 light-years across, compared with the Milky Way's diameter of 100,000 light-years. "This means the feedback is greatly enhanced," Silk says. "Our basic hypothesis is that the black holes really formed before most of the stars, and their vigorous outflows then created lots of stars. As time went on, this died away and led to the more conventional star formation that we have [today].

We think this is just a very special phenomenon that occurred early on and can explain the mysteries that we're seeing with JWST."

Fabio Pacucci of the Center for Astrophysics | Harvard & Smithsonian and his colleagues have studied the role black holes might have played at a later time in galaxies' evolution. In a galaxy like our own in the modern universe, the mass of stars outweighs the mass of the galaxy's central supermassive black hole—a feature that is ubiquitous among large galaxies—by a ratio of 1,000 to 1.

Using JWST to examine galaxies from 750 million to 1.5 billion years after the big bang, Pacucci found that some of them in this window may have a black hole whose mass matches their stellar mass—or perhaps even exceeds it. That points to a model of black hole growth in the early universe in which black holes grew from the direct collapse of clouds of dust and gas in the first 100 million years of the cosmos rather than from stars. This proposal is consistent with that of Silk and his colleagues and thus may bolster the astrophysical explanation of the rapid early growth of galaxies.

If that idea is correct, upcoming gravitational-wave observatories—such as the Laser Interferometer Space Antenna (LISA) space observatory, which was recently approved by the European Space Agency and is set for launch in 2035—might find these "heavy seed" black holes. "If these heavy seeds happened, then we would see a lot of mergers" with LISA, Pacucci says. "It's possible this will ease the problem of excessive mass."

There are ways to explain JWST's galaxies without black holes, too. Guochao Sun of Northwestern University and his colleagues have suggested that some galaxies in the universe might have gone through periods of "bursty" star formation. An abundance of supernovae could have temporarily led to a feedback process over 10 million years or so that increased star formation to rates "10 to 100 times" higher than those of more sedate galaxies, Sun says.

That could have caused the brightness of some galaxies in the early universe to "jump up and down very drastically," leading to a skewed sample of more visible bright galaxies. "You don't need to form stars at a very high efficiency," Sun adds. It may be that JWST's mysteriously bright early galaxies merely represent the upper end of dramatic fluctuations in star formation, with dimmer, more prosaic galaxies being more numerous but, so far, unseen.

Astrophysics, for the time being, reigns supreme. There is much at stake, however. "The fact that cosmology could be at play here means it's really worth following it up until it's excluded," Boylan-Kolchin says. Black holes and star formation are promising explanations, but scientists will be watching for fresh JWST results to see which, if any, of the new models hold firm.

About the Author

Jonathan O'Callaghan is an award-winning freelance journalist covering astronomy, astrophysics, commercial spaceflight and space exploration. Follow him on X @ Astro_Jonny

JWST's First Glimpses of Early Galaxies Could Break Cosmology

By Jonathan O'Callaghan

Rohan Naidu was at home with his girlfriend when he found the galaxy that nearly broke cosmology. As his algorithm dug through early images from the James Webb Space Telescope (JWST) late one night in July 2022, Naidu shot to attention. It had sifted out an object that Naidu recognized was inexplicably massive and dated back to just 300 million years after the big bang, making it older than any galaxy ever seen before. "I called my girlfriend over right away," Naidu says. "I told her, 'This might be the most distant starlight we've ever seen.'" After exchanging excited messages with one of his collaborators "with lots of exclamation marks," Naidu got to work. Days later they published a paper on the candidate galaxy, which they dubbed "GLASS-z13." The Internet exploded. "It reverberated around the world," Naidu says.

The discovery of this galaxy, just weeks into JWST's full operations, was beyond astronomers' wildest dreams. JWST—the largest, most powerful observatory ever launched from Earth—was built to revolutionize our understanding of the universe. Stationed 1.5 million kilometers away from earthly interference and chilled close to absolute zero by its tennis court–sized sunshade, the telescope's giant segmented mirror and exquisitely sensitive instruments were designed to uncover details of cosmic dawn never before observed.

This is the scarcely probed era—no more than a few hundred million years after the big bang itself—in which the very first stars and galaxies coalesced. How exactly this process unfolded depends on exotic physics, ranging from the uncertain influences of dark matter and dark energy to the poorly understood feedbacks between starlight, gas and dust. By glimpsing galaxies from cosmic dawn with JWST, cosmologists can test their knowledge of all these underlying phenomena–either confirming the validity of their best consensus models or revealing gaps in understanding that could herald profound new discoveries.

Such observations were supposed to take time; initial projections estimated the first galaxies would be so small and faint that JWST would find at best a few intriguingly remote candidates in its pilot investigations. Things didn't quite go as planned. Instead, as soon as the telescope's scientists released its very first images of the distant universe, astronomers such as Naidu (at the Massachusetts Institute of Technology) started finding numerous galaxies within them that, in apparent age, size and luminosity, surpassed all predictions. The competition for discovery was fierce: with each new day, it seemed, claims of yet another record-breaking "earliest known galaxy" emerged from one research group or another. "Everyone was freaking out," says Charlotte Mason, an astrophysicist at the University of Copenhagen. "We really weren't expecting this."

In the weeks and months following JWST's findings of surprisingly mature "early" galaxies, theorists and observers have been scrambling to explain them. Could the bevy of anomalously big and bright early galaxies be illusory, perhaps because of flaws in analysis of the telescope's initial observations? If genuine, could they somehow be explained by standard cosmological models? Or, just maybe, were they the first hints that the universe is more strange and complex than even our boldest theories had supposed?

At stake is nothing less than our very understanding of how the orderly universe we know emerged from primordial chaos. JWST's early revelations could rewrite the opening chapters of cosmic history, which concern not only distant epochs and faraway galaxies but also our own existence here in the familiar Milky Way. "You build these machines not to confirm the paradigm but to break it," says JWST scientist Mark McCaughrean, a senior adviser for science and exploration at the European Space Agency. "You just don't know how it will break."

Deep Looks for Cosmic Dawn

One might say JWST's observations of early galaxies have been billions of years in the making, but more modestly they trace back to the Space Telescope Science Institute (STScI) in 1985. At the time the Hubble Space Telescope was still five years away from launching on a space shuttle. But Garth Illingworth, then deputy director of the STScI, was surprised one day when his boss, then director Riccardo Giacconi, who died in 2018, asked him to start thinking about what would come after Hubble much farther down the road. "I protested, saying we've got more than enough to do on Hubble," Illingworth recalls. But Giacconi was insistent: "Trust me, it'll take a long time," he said. So, Illingworth and a handful of others got to work, drawing up concept ideas for what became known as the Next Generation Space Telescope (NGST), later renamed as JWST after a former NASA administrator.

Hubble would be transformational, but astronomers knew its capabilities would be limited by its observations in visible light. As light from a very distant galaxy travels across the cosmic abyss, it is stretched by the expansion of the universe—a broadening of wavelengths known as redshift. The higher the redshift value, the more stretching the light has experienced, and thus the more distant its source galaxy. Redshifts for early galaxies are so high that their emitted visible light has stretched into infrared by the time it arrives at our telescopes, which is why Hubble could not see them. The NGST, for comparison, would observe in infrared and would boast a very large (and very cold) starlight-gathering mirror, allowing it to peer much deeper into the universe. "Everybody realized that Webb would be the telescope for looking at early galaxies," Illingworth says. "That became the primary science goal."

The need for the telescope was highlighted in December 1995, when astronomers pointed Hubble at a seemingly empty patch of the sky for 10 consecutive days. Many experts predicted the extended observation would be a waste of resources, revealing at best a handful of dim galaxies, but instead the effort was richly rewarded. The resulting image, the Hubble Deep Field, showed the "empty" spot was filled with galaxies by the thousands, stretching back 12 billion years into the 13.8-billion-year history of our universe. "There were galaxies everywhere," says Illingworth, now an astrophysicist at the University of California, Santa Cruz. The Hubble Deep Field showed that the early universe was even more crowded and exciting than most anyone had expected, offering observational treasures to those who took the time and care to properly look. Yet, impressive as Hubble's Deep Field was, astronomers wanted more.

After more than two decades of labor at a cost of some $10 billion, JWST finally launched on Christmas Day 2021. The telescope reached its deep-space destination a month later, where it would endure exhaustive testing to ensure its optimal performance. By July 2022 it was ready to begin its long-awaited first year of science observations, known as Cycle 1. Part of the telescope's early time was devoted to high-impact programs across a range of disciplines from which data would immediately be made public. Two of those, CEERS (the Cosmic Evolution Early Release Science Survey) and GLASS (the Grism Lens–Amplified Survey from Space), independently spent dozens of hours looking for galaxies in the early universe by staring at separate small portions of the sky. Not much was expected—perhaps a slightly more ornate version of the Hubble Deep Field but nothing more. Steven Finkelstein of the University of Texas at Austin, the lead on CEERS, says extremely distant galaxies were predicted to pop up only "after a few cycles of data" from multiple programs.

Instead, much to the surprise of astronomers, extremely distant galaxies came into view immediately. Hubble's record for the most distant known galaxy had been GN-z11, spotted in 2015 at a redshift of 11 thanks to a 2009 upgrade that enhanced the telescope's modest infrared capabilities. A redshift of 11 corresponds to a cosmic age of about 400 million years, a point at the brink of when galaxy formation was thought to begin. But from the very first GLASS data, two teams—one led by Naidu in that breathless late-night discovery—independently found GLASS-z13 at a redshift of 13, some 70 million years farther back in time.

In their quest for quick results, the researchers relied on redshift estimates derived from simple brightness-based measurements. These are easier to obtain but less precise than direct measurements of redshift, which require more dedicated observation time. Nevertheless, the simplified technique can be accurate, and here it suggested a galaxy that was unexpectedly bright and big, already bearing a mass of stars equivalent to a billion suns, just a few hundred times less than that of the Milky Way's stellar population, despite our own galaxy being billions of years more mature. "This was beyond our most optimistic expectations," says Tommaso Treu, an astronomer at the University of California, Los Angeles, and the lead on GLASS.

The record didn't last long. In the following days, dozens of galaxy candidates from CEERS and GLASS sprang into view with estimated redshifts as high as 20—just 180 million years after the big bang—some with disklike structures that were not expected to manifest so early in cosmic history. Another team, meanwhile, found evidence for galaxies the size of our Milky Way at a redshift of 10, less than 500 million years after the big bang.

Such behemoths emerging so rapidly defies expectations set by cosmologists' standard model of the universe's evolution. Called Lambda CDM (LCDM), this model incorporates scientists' best estimates for the properties of dark energy and dark matter, which collectively act to dominate the emergence of large-scale cosmic structures. ("Lambda" refers to dark energy, and "CDM" refers to dark matter that is relatively sluggish, or "cold.") "Even if you took everything that was available to form stars and snapped your fingers instantaneously, you still wouldn't be able to get that big that early," says Michael Boylan-Kolchin, a cosmologist at the University of Texas at Austin. "It would be a real revolution."

How to Build a Galaxy

To understand the dilemma, a brief refresher is needed. In the first second after the big bang, our universe was an almost inconceivably hot and dense soup of primordial particles. Over the next three minutes, as the cosmos expanded and cooled, the nuclei of helium and other very light elements began to form. Fast-forward 400,000 years, and the universe was cold enough for the first atoms to appear. When the universe was about 100 million years old, theorists say, conditions were finally right for the emergence of the first stars. These giant fireballs of mostly hydrogen and helium were uncontaminated by heavier elements found in modern-day stars, so they possessed significantly different properties. Larger and brighter than today's stars, these first suns coalesced in protogalaxies–clusters of gas that clung to vast, invisible scaffolds of dark matter. Gravity guided the subsequent interactions between these protogalaxies, which eventually merged to form larger galaxies. This process of becoming, of the early universe's chaos giving way to the more orderly cosmos we know today, is thought to have taken about a billion years.

JWST's discovery of bright galaxies in the early cosmos challenges this model. "We should see lots of these little protogalactic fragments that have not yet merged to make a big galaxy," says Stacy McGaugh, a cosmologist at Case Western Reserve University. "Instead we're seeing a few things that are already big galaxies." Some of these galaxies may be impostors, much closer galaxies shrouded in dust that makes them look dimmer and farther away when brightness-based measurements are used. Follow-up observations of GLASS-z13 in August 2022 by the Atacama Large Millimeter Array (ALMA) in Chile, however, suggest that is not the case for this candidate, because ALMA did not see evidence for large amounts of dust. "I think we can exclude low-redshift interlopers," says Tom Bakx, an astronomer at Nagoya University in Japan, who led the observations. Yet the lack of dust means ALMA struggled to see the galaxy at all, showing how difficult it could be for telescopes to confirm observations made using

JWST's advanced capabilities. "The good news is there's nothing detected," Naidu says. "The bad news is there's nothing detected." Only JWST, in this case, can follow up itself.

The most startling explanation is that the canonical LCDM cosmological model is wrong and requires revision. "These results are very surprising and hard to get in our standard model of cosmology," Boylan-Kolchin says. "And it's probably not a small change. We'd have to go back to the drawing board." One controversial idea is modified Newtonian dynamics (MOND), which posits that dark matter does not exist and that its effects can instead be explained by large-scale fluctuations in gravity. To date, JWST's observations could support such a theory. "MOND has had a lot of its predictions come true–this is another one of them," says McGaugh, who is one of the idea's leading proponents. Others remain unconvinced. "So far everything that we've tried to test MOND hasn't been able to really provide a satisfactory answer," says Jeyhan Kartaltepe, an astrophysicist at the Rochester Institute of Technology.

One simpler solution is that galaxies in the early universe could have little or no dust, making them appear brighter. This scenario could confound efforts to calculate the galaxies' true masses and could perhaps also explain ALMA's difficulty spotting GLASS-z13. "It could be that supernovae didn't have enough time to produce the dust, or maybe in the initial phases [of galaxy formation] the dust is expelled from galaxies," says Andrea Ferrara, an astronomer at the Scuola Normale Superiore in Italy, who has proposed such a possibility. Alternatively, Mason and her colleagues suggest that in its observations of the early universe JWST may so far be seeing only the very brightest young galaxies, as they should be the easiest to spot. "Maybe there's something happening in the early universe that means it's easier for some galaxies to form stars," she says.

David Spergel, a theoretical astrophysicist and current president of the Simons Foundation in New York City, agrees. "I think what we're seeing is that high-mass star formation is very efficient in the early universe," he says. "The gas pressures are higher. The temperatures are higher. That has an enormous impact on the environment for star formation." Magnetic fields might have arisen earlier in the universe than we thought, driving material to kick-start the birth of stars. "We might be seeing a signature of magnetic fields emerging very early in the universe's history," Spergel says.

A Rush to Break the Universe

The rapid flow of scientific papers from JWST's initial observations is no fluke; when the first data arrived, astronomers were eagerly waiting. "People had been working on their pipelines for years," Boylan-Kolchin says. Instead of the traditional peer-review process, which can take months, astronomers published on arXiv, a website where scientific papers can be uploaded after minimal review by moderators but well before formal peer review. This new form of review is unfolding in near real time on X (formerly Twitter) and other social media platforms. "It's science by arXiv," Naidu says. The resulting frenzy was intense–and surprising. "I expected a lot of activity," says Nancy Levenson, STScI's interim director. "But I underestimated the amount."

The result was that scientific results could be rapidly publicized and discussed, but some fear at a cost. "People were rushing things a little bit," says Klaus Pontoppidan, JWST's project scientist at STScI. "The gold standard is a refereed, peer-reviewed paper." Early calibration issues with JWST, for example, may have affected some results. Nathan Adams of the University of Manchester in England and his colleagues found there could be dramatic changes, with one galaxy at a redshift of 20.4 recalibrated to a redshift of just 0.7. "We need to calm down a little bit," Adams says. "It's a bit too early to say we've completely broken the universe."

Such issues are unlikely to eradicate all of JWST's high-redshift galaxies, however, given their sheer number. "It's more likely that the early universe is different from what we predicted," Finkelstein says. "The odds are small that we're all wrong." Astronomers are now racing to conduct follow-up observations with JWST. Levenson says she's currently reviewing about a dozen proposals from various groups asking for additional JWST observing time, most of which are seeking to scrutinize high-redshift galaxy candidates. "Considering the excitement and importance of these early discoveries, we thought it was appropriate to ask for a little bit of time to confirm them," says Treu, who put forward one of the proposals.

More programs have been designed to hunt for distant galaxies, such as COSMOS-Webb, co-led by Kartaltepe, which aims to hugely increase the known population of early galaxies by observing a wider swath of sky for hundreds of hours. "We estimate there are thousands we'll be able to detect," she says. Future proposals might look for evidence of those first protogalaxies, perhaps using the explosive deaths of supersized first stars in especially luminous and energetic supernovae as markers for their existence. Some estimates suggest JWST could see as far as a redshift of 26, just 120 million years after the big bang, a cosmic blink of an eye. Much other work will be done to follow up the growing list of high-redshift candidates. "Even confirming a handful of these would be quite amazing," Naidu says. "It would demonstrate we're not getting fooled."

JWST has ushered in a new era of science, and despite the uncertainties, the rapid communication of new discoveries has invigorated astronomers. "It's been fantastic," Treu says. "It's really wonderful to see the community so engaged and excited." Now the question is, If we can truly believe what we are seeing, is it time to reappraise our understanding of the dawn of time? "We're peering into the unknown," Mason says.

About the Author

Jonathan O'Callaghan is an award-winning freelance journalist covering astronomy, astrophysics, commercial spaceflight and space exploration. Follow him on X @ Astro_Jonny

Astronomers Grapple with JWST's Discovery of Early Galaxies

By Jonathan O'Callaghan

In their quest to understand the first stars and galaxies that lit up the cosmos, astronomers are still in the dark–but getting closer to enlightenment one discovery at a time.

That's the almost inescapable conclusion from initial observations by the James Webb Space Telescope (JWST), the $10-billion observatory that began science operations in July. Designed to glimpse the faint infrared glow of the universe's earliest luminous objects, JWST's vision reaches back into the first few hundred million years after the big bang, allowing it to obtain more and better data about newborn galaxies than any other facility yet built. But its haul of galactic "baby pictures" has proved more bountiful than most researchers dared to dream. Simply put, candidate galaxies in the early universe are popping up in numbers that defy predictions, with dozens found so far. Explaining this excess may require substantial revisions to prevailing cosmological models, changes that could involve the first galaxies forming sooner, their stars shining brighter–or perhaps the nature of dark matter or dark energy being even more complex and mysterious than previously thought.

Now two of JWST's most tantalizing candidate early galaxies have stood up to further scrutiny, strengthening scientists' suspicions that our knowledge of cosmic history is crucially incomplete. Dating back to 350 million and 450 million years after the big bang, at the time of their discovery, both galaxies were older than any others known before. They were found independently by two teams, one led by Rohan Naidu, now at the Massachusetts Institute of Technology, and the other led by Marco Castellano of the Astronomical Observatory of Rome in Italy. Initially posted on the preprint server arXiv.org, the two discovery papers have now cleared the key hurdle of peer-reviewed publication, each appearing in the *Astrophysical Journal*

Letters in late November and October, respectively. This is more than a ceremonial milestone—early calibration issues with JWST's instruments had fueled concerns among astronomers that such findings had potentially miscalculated the true distance to these galaxies, making them more modern imposters only appearing to be part of the early cosmic coterie. But after thorough peer review, "we can say with very good confidence that calibration is not an issue for these galaxies," Castellano says. "They are very robust candidates. We have finally put to the rest the issues with calibration." Follow-up observations will be needed, however, to absolutely confirm their record-breaking distances.

Astronomers have meanwhile since found several other early galaxy candidates, some seemingly as far back as 200 million years post–big bang. Prior to the launch of JWST, no one knew if galaxies could even form so early in the universe's 13.8-billion-year history, at a time when matter was thought to still be sedately coalescing into the gravitationally bound clumps required to give birth to large groups of stars. "And so we're wondering, 'Do we really understand the early phases of the formation of these galaxies?'" said Garth Illingworth, an astronomer at the University of California, Santa Cruz, at a press conference held by NASA to announce the peer-reviewed validation of the first two candidates. "This has posed a lot of questions for the theorists."

Chief among them is how, exactly, dark matter guided the emergence of galaxies. For the first few hundred thousand years after the big bang, the cosmos was so hot that gravity could not pull normal matter together to form large protogalactic clumps. Yet this was "not an issue for dark matter," says Jorge Peñarrubia, a cosmologist at the University of Edinburgh in Scotland, "because dark matter does not interact via electromagnetic forces." Instead gravity alone is this invisible substance's master—meaning that in mere moments after the big bang, when primordial chaos otherwise reigned, gravity immediately began glomming together dark matter into large clumps known as halos. These dark matter halos are believed to have acted as gravitational sinks for normal matter, seeding the subsequent formation of galaxies in the early universe. The telltale motions of the stars they shepherd betray their endurance to this day. Such halos still surround galaxies like our own, majestic-but-invisible sculptors of the modern cosmos.

JWST's rapid discovery of early galaxies might be testing our understanding of how these halos form, perhaps suggesting they reached an immense bulk earlier than expected. One explanation might involve the very nature of dark matter itself. Theorists have found that simple treatments of dark matter, in which it only interacts with itself and normal matter via gravity, can accurately replicate large-scale cosmic structure. But nature has no guarantee of simplicity. In reality, dark matter could interact with itself because of an as yet unknown force, perhaps via a particle that's not in the current Standard Model of physics—possibly increasing the speed at which these halos grew and explaining how big, bright galaxies were able to arise so quickly.

Perhaps instead, however, these halos were simply more efficient at drawing in regular matter to feed star formation. "I think this is probably telling us something about how stars form in dark matter halos early on," Peñarrubia says. Today our galaxy produces roughly one new star per year, but Castellano's paper suggests that star-formation rates must have been at least 20 times higher in his and Naidu's two candidate galaxies. Another JWST-derived preprint paper posits that Milky Way–sized galaxies could have arisen just a half-billion years after the big bang—a scenario that would demand star-formation rates 10 times higher still than Castellano's estimates. But according to Michael Boylan-Kolchin, a cosmologist at the University of Texas at Austin, such outsize rates of star formation stretch the boundaries of what is physically possible. "If those values are correct, you'd need to have [galaxies] turning all their mass into stars and forming stars as fast as they could," he says.

A perhaps more plausible possibility is that stars were somehow more efficient at accumulating mass in the early universe. This would lead to bulkier, brighter stars, enhancing early galaxies' visibility to JWST. "Maybe you just create a whole load of very,

very massive stars," says Stephen Wilkins, an astronomer at the University of Sussex in England. These could be so-called Population III stars, the hypothesized first stars in the universe. Although astronomers have yet to conclusively observe such stars, there is plentiful circumstantial evidence for their existence. Emerging from the primordial hydrogen and helium gas that pervaded the early universe, Population III stars would lack heavier elements, allowing them to reach humongous sizes–hundreds of times bulkier than our sun. But like the brightest, briefest candles, these stars' immensity would limit their lifetime to no more than a few million years, making their detection today difficult.

It is possible, however, that some of the more remote galaxies already found by JWST–and those even more ancient that may still await discovery–could contain evidence for Population III stars. The brightness of these galaxies could be attributed to such stars, which would be much hotter and brighter than subsequent Population II stars and Population I stars, such as our sun, both of which fill our modern-day universe. "It's very definitely possible," says Daniel Whalen, a cosmologist at the University of Portsmouth in England. To find out for certain, JWST will need to perform spectroscopic follow-up of these more distant galaxy candidates–a time-consuming process of gathering a rainbowlike spectrum from a galaxy's emitted light to work out which chemical elements are present in its constituent stars. One clear signature of Population III stars, Whalen says, could be a specific spectral feature of helium that could only arise within stars that are hotter than about 100,000 degrees Celsius. "That would be evidence for a massive Population III star," he says.

Such follow-up observations are set to begin imminently. Jeyhan Kartaltepe of the Rochester Institute of Technology is part of a team that has been approved time on JWST to follow up a handful of early galaxy candidates found in the Cosmic Evolution Early Release Science (CEERS) Survey, for which Kartaltepe is a leading investigator. Such candidates are distinguished by their high redshifts–a stretching out of the wavelengths of their light caused by the expansion of the universe across cosmic time. This makes Kartaltepe's spectroscopic follow-up not only an important probe of the galaxies' stellar populations but also yet another "reality check" of their cosmic vintage. The hope is the measurements will allow astronomers to "understand the star formation rates and the age of the stars," Kartaltepe says. The program, expected to begin no sooner than late December, will use eight hours of JWST time to obtain spectra of three target galaxies. Many more such programs are expected in the future.

Other, more intriguing ideas abound. If JWST finds that the apparent early burst of massive galaxy formation suddenly ebbed in subsequent cosmic epochs, this could suggest the universe was expanding faster than expected back then—perhaps twice as fast as predicted by current consensus estimates, says Nicola Menci, an astronomer at the Astronomical Observatory of Rome. This could be linked to the influence of a particular (and so far entirely hypothetical) variety of dark energy, which is the enigmatic and mysterious force that appears to drive the accelerating expansion of the universe. So-called phantom models of dark energy allow its potency to fluctuate across cosmic time. If such models are valid, they suggest dark energy's influence on the universe's expansion could have been far greater shortly after the big bang than they are today. Initial results from JWST "seem to be in contrast with most logical models we have considered up to now," Menci says, namely Lambda Cold Dark Matter (Lambda-CDM), the theoretical model incorporating cosmologists' current best estimates for the properties of dark matter and dark energy and their resulting effects on cosmic evolution.

Such ideas, while seemingly far-fetched, cannot yet be entirely ruled out as astronomers continue to grapple with the prevalence of galaxy candidates in the early universe. Some will likely turn out to be mirages, much closer galaxies masquerading as more remote ones because they contain large amounts of dust, which also causes their light to be redshifted. Yet initial follow-up of one of Castellano's and Naidu's galaxies using the Atacama Large Millimeter/submillimeter

Array (ALMA) in Chile suggested little evidence for such high dust content. "Despite the ALMA results being interesting, JWST is the only instrument that can give definitive answers on these galaxies," however, Castellano says.

Additional follow-up observations of galaxies like these may be conducted in JWST's first year of science, Cycle 1, which runs until June 2023.More interesting results may occur in its second year of science, Cycle 2, for which astronomers can now propose programs by a deadline of January 27, 2023. "Spectroscopic follow-up with JWST is essential and is likely to dominate the requests on distant galaxies in Cycle 2," Illingworth says. "We have a problem, and it's real: Where the hell did these bright things come from? They weren't in the storybook. We really have to understand what's going on here."

About the Author

Jonathan O'Callaghan is an award-winning freelance journalist covering astronomy, astrophysics, commercial spaceflight and space exploration. Follow him on X @ Astro_Jonny

JWST's Newfound Galaxies Are the Oldest Ever Seen

By Jonathan O'Callaghan

In a cosmological matchup of "Are they or aren't they?" the contest is firmly in the former's favor—10 to one, at last count. The question is one of profound importance: Are the galaxies the James Webb Space Telescope (JWST) is seeing in the early universe really as astonishingly remote as we think they are? So far, the answer is a resounding yes. "The vast majority of these galaxies are being confirmed," says Steven Finkelstein, an astronomer at the University of Texas at Austin. "It means that everything we saw last summer, that maybe the universe was very proficient at forming stars very early, is going to stand."

The summer of 2022 saw JWST unleash a torrent of discoveries. After a launch in December 2021 and more than half a year of commissioning, JWST fully switched on in July 2022. Almost immediately thereafter, its unprecedented infrared sensitivity revealed the faint glows of galaxies apparently from the far-distant universe that had formed just hundreds of millions of years after the big bang. Astronomers had expected such landmark results to emerge more gradually. "There was an explosion of data," Finkelstein says.

Those early results came about so quickly because researchers used a clever shortcut to estimate galactic distances. Astronomers usually pin down cosmic coordinates via precisely measuring redshift, a stretching of a galaxy's light toward the red end of the electromagnetic spectrum as a result of the universe's expansion. But this requires the act of assembling and analyzing a galaxy's spectrum—a time-consuming and subtle process known as spectroscopy. JWST's firehose of discovery was instead powered by cruder, faster photometry-based techniques that essentially use obvious variations in galaxies' brightness to estimate their redshift.

Thus, while the photometric results came thick and fast last summer, the spectroscopic results have only just begun trickling out. Already, though, with spectra-based distances in hand from only about a dozen candidates, researchers are finding that most measurements are matching the early photometric results. The latest, published in *Nature Astronomy* last week, confirm earlier distance estimates for four more galaxies identified by the JWST Advanced Deep Extragalactic Survey (JADES). "We've been waiting decades for this," says Emma Curtis-Lake of the University of Hertfordshire in England, who led the spectroscopic results study. "To be able to do it within the first few months of this telescope was just incredible."

Of the four, the most distant is one with the somewhat unwieldy name JADES-GS-z13-0. It has a redshift value of 13.2, meaning we are seeing the galaxy as it appeared just 320 million years after the big bang. That high redshift makes JADES-GS-z13-0 the most distant currently known in the universe—a record that JWST seems set to imminently break again but one that highlights why astronomers are so thrilled. We now know for certain we are probing an era of the universe no human has ever laid eyes on before. "It's astonishing," says Pieter van Dokkum of Yale University. This galaxy, he evocatively notes, is only slightly older from our perspective than the total time sharks have existed on Earth—some 300 million years. "You go from nothing to these fully formed galaxies in the blink of an eye," van Dokkum says.

Not all high-redshift candidate galaxies have been so lucky, however, which highlights astronomers' early caution. In July another survey called the Cosmic Evolution Early Release Science Survey (CEERS), led by Finkelstein, spied a possible galaxy at a redshift of 16.4, just 240 million years after the big bang. Subsequent spectroscopy has shown that deduction was wrong, as revealed in late March in research led by Pablo Arrabal Haro, an astronomer at the National Science Foundation's NOIRLab. The galaxy is actually a dusty imposter located at a redshift of 4.9, a still impressive but not at all record-breaking 1.2 billion years after the big bang. High levels of star formation are thought to have muddled early photometric analysis. "We can be easily fooled by contamination," says Callum Donnan of the University of Edinburgh in Scotland, a co-author on the work. "A high-redshift galaxy can be mimicked by a lower-redshift galaxy with different features."

The good news is that this particular galaxy appears to be a "unique case," Donnan says. The same study was able to confirm that two other candidate galaxies did not have the same problem. One of these is Maisie's galaxy, which is seen at a redshift of 11.4, about 400 million years after the big bang, and was named for Finkelstein's daughter. "She was very excited when I told her it was real," Finkelstein says.

Now that such galaxies are being confirmed, their scientific implications can be more fully explored. These galaxies are small, many times tinier than the Milky Way. But some appear extremely bright and massive and have high star formation rates similar to that of our galaxy, which forms roughly one new star every year. While the galaxies don't yet pose problems for leading models of cosmology, they suggest galactic formation began earlier and proceeded faster than expected in the universe, which theorists had previously predicted began churning out galaxies at the ripe age of one billion years after the big bang.

"We're seeing a rise of massive galaxies faster than we thought previously," says Fabio Pacucci of the Harvard-Smithsonian Center for Astrophysics. The ages of some of these early galaxies are estimated at just tens of millions of years. This could have implications for large structures of dark matter known as halos that sculpted early galaxies and for the nature of dark matter particles themselves. "One of the big open questions is: What is dark matter?" says Sandro Tacchella of the University of Cambridge. "The first generation of galaxies is a sensitive probe for different dark matter models."

Some problematic—and potentially model-busting—early-universe candidate galaxies still remain. First among them may be a class of galaxies identified by Ivo Labbé of the Swinburne University of Technology in Australia and his colleagues. The team found galaxies with billions of solar masses, comparable in weight to the Milky Way, from just an estimated 750 million years after the big bang. These galaxies are 10 to 100 times bigger than galaxies previously seen in this era and are packed into structures 30 times smaller than the Milky Way. "They're small, but they're massive," says Labbé, who says JWST is continuing to find similar galaxies essentially anywhere it looks deeply in the sky. For now the galaxies have only been studied by photometry, with spectroscopic analysis planned for July. But the photometric success of other JWST results so far suggests Labbé and his colleagues' preliminary analysis is correct. "The most extreme galaxies there still seem to pose a problem," says Michael Boylan-Kolchin of the University of Texas at Austin, who was not involved in the JWST observations discussed in this article. "Some of these systems would have to be forming stars 1,000 times as fast as the Milky Way. The question is: Is that an impossibly high amount of star formation?"

The field continues to change rapidly. An ongoing survey called COSMOS-Webb is expected to deliver many more high-redshift candidates. "Our estimates in the proposal were [to find galaxies] up to a redshift of 10 or so," says Jeyhan Kartaltepe of the Rochester Institute of Technology, who leads the program. "But those numbers might have been too pessimistic." Many other astronomers have submitted requests for additional spare time on the telescope to the Space Telescope Science Institute in Maryland, which runs the observatory. More still have submitted proposals for the telescope's second year of scheduled scientific observations, called Cycle 2, which begins in July.

Some worry the field is moving too fast. While many of JWST's data, about 80 percent, have a proprietary window of 12 months in which the researchers responsible have exclusive access to their own observations, the rest are open-access. This means that when observations are taken, they are immediately accessible to the public, and anyone can use them. Before Arrabal Haro and his colleagues had published their analysis of the redshift 16.4 galaxy on the preprint server arXiv.org in late March, their open-access work had already been scooped by astronomers on Twitter. "I wanted to do just an extremely simple test," says Gabriel Brammer of the University of Copenhagen, who posted some of the early results. "The team did a much more detailed analysis. But you can see it instantly if you know where to look."

Not everyone is happy with such easy access. "You have postdocs who have spent years of their life working on this and making these observations possible," says Rebecca Larson of U.T. Austin, a co-author of Arrabal Haro's paper and part of the CEERS team. "Then our data comes out, and it's public, and people are racing us to the results. We are working on it and also being asked to provide other input for the community. Then other people will come in and put up papers. It's really frustrating to watch happen." It is unclear how to resolve the tensions at the moment. "It'd be better if there were some more concrete rules," says Tom Bakx of Nagoya University in Japan, who was not involved in the research. "Imagine if you have small kids, then it's simply not possible to spend the entire night calibrating the data. There's a little bit of a power imbalance. It's very open competition."

More positively, the situation appears to have cooled somewhat since the frenetic early weeks of JWST's operation. Now astronomers are doing what they long dreamed of–gaining their first certain glimpses into an epoch of the universe never studied before. Who knows how much further we will see. "Maybe galaxy formation started already at a redshift of 20," van Dokkum says, referring to a time a mere 180 million years after the big bang, an epoch scarcely fathomable prior to JWST. If the telescope is showing us anything, however, it's to expect the unexpected.

About the Author

Jonathan O'Callaghan is an award-winning freelance journalist covering astronomy, astrophysics, commercial spaceflight and space exploration. Follow him on X @ Astro_Jonny

How Can Galaxies Ever Collide in an Ever-Expanding Universe?

By Phil Plait

I get e-mail.

Most messages are press releases about astronomical discoveries–okay, scratch that; *most* of them are spam, but science announcements are an easy second place. But I also get questions from readers asking about various aspects of the universe that they're struggling to understand.

I love this! For one thing, it shows that people really are curious about science, and you have to dig that. For another, it gives me a chance to explain counterintuitive concepts that are probably bugging other people as well.

One perennial question I get concerns cosmology (an understandably puzzling topic): If the universe is expanding, how can galaxies collide? Shouldn't they be flying away from each other, not *toward* one another?

There are actually two reasons galaxies can collide in an expanding cosmos. One is that the expansion only dominates on very large scales, and the other is that the expansion competes against gravity.

Okay, first thing first: the universe is in fact expanding. We've known this for more than a century now, and it's the basis for modern cosmology. This idea is called the big bang model–which is an unfortunate name because it brings to mind a cosmos expanding like an explosion, with galaxies moving away from each other through space like shrapnel.

But in fact *space itself is expanding*, and that's different. It's not that galaxies are moving through space; it's that the expansion of space is carrying them along with it. This has a lot of deeply strange implications. One is that the farther away a galaxy is from us, the faster it appears to be receding.

Imagine a meterstick that's made of some extremely flexible material. The two endpoints are, of course, one meter apart. At the center, you can mark two points that are one centimeter apart.

Now grab each end of this pretend meterstick and stretch them out so that the stick is now two meters long. (Ask an imaginary friend for help.) The two endpoints have moved a meter farther apart, traveling at, say, one meter per second. But those marks you made earlier that were one centimeter apart are now two centimeters apart because the whole meterstick stretched. That means those two points moved away from each other at a velocity of only one centimeter per second, much slower than the endpoints. In other words, *the farther away two points are in an expanding scale, the faster they move away from each other.*

That's the universe in a nutshell. We see more distant galaxies receding from us more rapidly, and we can even measure that change of velocity over distance. Very roughly speaking, for every megaparsec in distance (3.26 million light-years, a convenient unit for astronomers but not for anyone else), space is expanding at an additional 70 or so kilometers per second. So a galaxy that's, say, 10 megaparsecs away from us is receding at about 700 km/sec.

That's pretty fast. But a galaxy one megaparsec away is only moving away at 70 km/sec. While that's still speedy—a quarter of a million km/hour!—it's possible for galaxies to travel faster than that *through* space, shrapnel-style.

The Andromeda galaxy offers a great example. It's the closest large spiral to our Milky Way, and we both belong to a regional clump of galaxies called the Local Group. At 2.5 million light-years from us, Andromeda should be receding at 50 km/sec or so, but in fact it is heading our way at approximately 110 km/sec. This is because both galaxies are close enough together that each is pulled by the gravity of the other—pulled so hard, in fact, that their mutual velocity is far larger than the universe's ability to pry them apart. This is also why Andromeda and the Milky Way may someday collide and even merge, though not for perhaps another eight billion years.

And this brings us to the second reason galaxies can still collide in an expanding universe. We think of gravity as a force pulling things together. But according to Einstein's general theory of relativity, gravity is actually a bending of spacetime, like a dimple in a sheet. If an object passes by something with a lot of mass, such as a planet or a galaxy, that warping causes the object's path to bend, to curve.

If two objects have sufficient mass and are moving at relatively slow speeds, they can be gravitationally bound, meaning their velocities can't overcome gravity, and they stay close together in what's called a closed orbit. A moon orbiting a planet is like that—or two galaxies, such as the Milky Way and Andromeda.

This is where things get weird. According to relativity, if space is expanding, it *cannot* expand inside that bound region. The mutual gravity of the objects inside that region holds them together; space expands around that volume but not inside it. That, in turn, means if two galaxies swoop sufficiently close together, they can still collide. For a deeper dive into this (so to speak!), my colleague and fellow science writer Ethan Siegel has written about this as well.

It gets even weirder than this, however, because we now know the expansion of the universe isn't constant. In 1998 two teams of astronomers announced that the expansion is accelerating, getting faster all the time, caused by a still-mysterious entity called dark energy. This could mean, for some still-theorized behaviors of dark energy, that even space inside a bound region can expand. This effect would be strongest over the largest-distance scales, so, for example, the slowest-moving galaxies near the edge of a galaxy cluster would be lost to the expansion, stripped away from the cluster like the outermost leaves on a head of lettuce.

Given enough time and incessant cosmic acceleration, *every* bound structure would get ripped apart—even ones bound by forces other than gravity, like molecules and even atoms themselves! Astronomers call this idea the big rip, for obvious enough reasons, and it's not a very reassuring fate. But we really don't know what dark energy is or how it behaves over long periods of time, so the big rip is only one possible scenario for the extremely distant future.

So don't worry: whether we're talking about the big rip or a collision with Andromeda, the timescales at play are so immense that these events won't happen for eons (if at all), so they don't really affect your daily life—unless you're an astronomer, in which case they *do*. But we enjoy thinking about such things and relaying those thoughts to you. Hopefully they'll help expand your mind.

About the Author

Phil Plait is a professional astronomer and science communicator in Virginia. His column for Scientific American, *The Universe, covers all things space. He writes the* Bad Astronomy Newsletter. *Follow him online.*

Astronomers Witness the Birth of a New Solar System

By Joseph Howlett

Planets around other stars can help answer one of the greatest mysteries: How did we get here? How did the spinning disk of material left behind by our sun's birth form our planet and its seven neighbors? Typically astronomers find planets of similar ages to the ones in our solar system, but that's starting to change.

In a study published today in the *Astrophysical Journal Letters*, astronomers reveal a baby solar system forming around a star some 437 light-years from Earth–it is only the second ever to be confirmed. The first, PDS 70, was discovered in 2018.

"This is a really exciting discovery," says Jason Wang, an astronomer at Northwestern University who wasn't involved in the research. "In astronomy, we often joke that when we have a sample size of one, we have an anomaly, but when we have a sample size of two, we have a population."

Some of the astronomers behind the new study revealed last year that the star, called WISPIT 2, had a protoplanet forming around it, WISPIT 2b. It marked the first time a baby planet had been imaged in a protoplanetary disk. Now they believe there are two gas giant planets, with the second about 10 times the size of Jupiter.

And the authors think there are more protoplanets to find around WISPIT 2. The star appears to be surrounded by a more extensive, structured ring of matter than PDS 70. And further out in the disk, the astronomers have spotted a third, smaller break in the material–a tantalizing hint that matter there may have already collapsed into a planet closer to Saturn's size. The new finding was made using the European Southern Observatory's Very Large Telescope in Chile's Atacama Desert, and the authors hope that its successor, the Extremely Large Telescope, will be able to snap photos of the third hypothetical infant.

"These structures suggest that more planets are currently forming, which we will eventually detect," says Chloe Lawlor, a Ph.D. student at the University of Galway in Ireland and the study's lead author. By studying this new planetary nursery and others like it, astronomers hope to get a tighter grasp on how our own solar system came to be.

For her part, Lawlor is surprised to have led such a groundbreaking study as a young scientist. "Often there is a lot of self-doubt for people at my career stage," she says. "I hope this discovery helps others to realize that while they might not know it all yet, they still know enough to do big things."

About the Author

Joseph Howlett is a staff reporter at Scientific American *covering physics, math, astronomy and more. He was previously a math staff writer at* Quanta Magazine, *and holds a Ph.D. in particle physics from Columbia University.*

GLOSSARY

accretion The gradual increase of material on the outside of an object.

barycenter The center of mass around which two objects orbit.

decommissioned A system that's been taken out of service.

enigma A situation or thing that's difficult to understand.

exomoon A natural satellite that orbits a planet outside our solar system.

exoplanet A planet that orbits a star outside our solar system.

exorings Rings that orbit an exoplanet.

geocentrism An outdated view that puts Earth at the center of the universe.

incandescent To produce a bright light by heating to a high temperature.

ionized The process of knocking electrons off of atoms and turning them into charged particles.

kinetically Characterized by energy and motion.

microlensing When an object (lens) passes in front of a star (source), which causes the source's light to temporarily brighten and bend.

parable A short story used to teach a lesson.

photons A tiny particle of light and other forms of electromagnetic radiation.

polarization The process of separating something into two opposing groups.

soupçon A very small amount of something added to something else.

torus A 3D shape with a single hole, such as a donut or tube.

FURTHER INFORMATION

Furfaro, Emily. "How Big is Space? We Asked a NASA Expert: Episode: 61." NASA. May 21, 2025. www.nasa.gov/science-research/astrophysics/how-big-is-space-we-asked-a-nasa-expert-episode-61/.

Gunn, Alastair. "How Big Is the Universe? This Is What Astronomers Think the Size of the Cosmos Is, and How They Worked It Out." *BBC Sky at Night Magazine*. August 29, 2025. /www.skyatnightmagazine.com/space-science/how-big-universe.

Krywko, Jacek. "'Inside-Out' Planetary System Perplexes Astronomers." *Scientific American*. February 12, 2026. www.scientificamerican.com/article/inside-out-planetary-system-perplexes-astronomers/.

Lee, Gayoung. "This Supermassive Black Hole May Harbor a Bizarre Star That Refuses to Die." *Scientific American*. January 17, 2025. www.scientificamerican.com/article/this-supermassive-black-hole-may-harbor-a-bizarre-undead-star/.

Plait, Phil. "Have Astronomers Found a Runaway Monster Black Hole or Just a Very Weird Galaxy?" *Scientific American*. March 13, 2026. www.scientificamerican.com/article/have-astronomers-found-a-runaway-monster-black-hole/.

Siegel, Ethan. "Ask Ethan: How Can We Comprehend the Size of the Universe?" Big Think. January 13, 2023. bigthink.com/starts-with-a-bang/comprehend-size-universe/.

Sottosanti, Karen. "Observable Universe." *Britannica*. www.britannica.com/topic/observable-universe.

Tremblay, Robert. "The Scale of the Universe." Vatican Observatory. August 11, 2018. www.vaticanobservatory.org/sacred-space-astronomy/the-scale-of-the-universe-re-run/.

CITATIONS

Content originally published on or after July 1, 2018, was reproduced with permission. Copyright 2027 Scientific American, a Division of Springer Nature America, Inc. All rights reserved.

Content originally published from January 1, 2010 to June 30, 2018, was reproduced with permission. Copyright 2027 Scientific American, a Division of Nature America, Inc. All rights reserved.

Content originally published on or before December 31, 2009, was reproduced with permission. Copyright 2027 Scientific American, Inc. All rights reserved.

1.1 Jupiter Isn't as Huge as We Thought It Was by Jackie Flynn Mogensen (February 2, 2026); 1.2 Another Earth or a Blip in the Data? We May Never Find Out by Joseph Howlett (January 30, 2026); 1.3 Scientists Just Clocked a 'Rogue' Planet the Size of Saturn by Jackie Flynn Mogensen (January 1, 2026); 1.4 How Far are We from Finding Exomoons and Exorings? by Phil Plait (February 27, 2026); 2.1 The Universe Is Static. No, Expanding! Wait, Slowing? Oh, Accelerating by Richard Panek (August 19, 2025); 2.2 The James Webb Space Telescope Could Solve One of Cosmology's Deepest Mysteries by Daniel Leonard (January 25, 2022); 2.3 Physicists Propose a Simpler, Hotter Origin for the Cosmos by Stephanie Pappas (October 28, 2025); 2.4 AI Reveals 800 Never-Before-Seen "Cosmic Anomalies" in Old Hubble Images by Jackie Flynn Mogensen (January 27, 2026); 2.5 Astronomers Are Agog over This All-Day Gamma-Ray Burst by Yvette Cendes (November 5, 2025); 3.1 How Big Can a Black Hole Be? by Phil Plait (September 5, 2025); 3.2 Hypervelocity Stars Hint at a Supermassive Black Hole Right Next Door by Phil Plait (May 23, 2025); 3.3 3,000-Light-Year-Long Jet Offers New Clues to First Black Hole Ever Imaged by Jackie Flynn Mogensen (January 30, 2026); 3.4 Back From the Dead, a Black Hole is Erupting After a 100-Million-Year Hiatus by K. R. Callaway (January 24, 2026); 3.5 "Little Red Dots" Spied by JWST May Be Baby Black Holes in Disguise by Lee Billings (January 15, 2026); 3.6 Could Colossal Black Hole Jets Have Shaped the Early Universe? by Saima S. Iqbal (October 23, 2024); 3.7 Weird, Wobbling Black Hole Jets Can Shape Entire Galaxies by Jacek Krywko (January 8, 2026); 3.8 Our Galaxy's Biggest Black Hole Just Got a New Close-up. What's Next Could Be Even Wilder by Michael Greshko (April 16, 2024); 3.9 The Milky Way's Central Black Hole May Have Appeared Shockingly Different Just a Few Hundred Years Ago by Jackie Flynn Mogensen (January 13, 2026); 3.10 Black Hole Caught Blasting Matter into Space at 130 Million MPH by Claire Cameron (December 9, 2025); 4.1 When Will We See the Universe's First Stars? by José María Diego Rodríguez (January 20, 2026); 4.2 The Pleiades Star Cluster Has a Secret Stellar Family Scattered across the Milky Way by Phil Plait (January 2, 2026); 4.3 What's the Most Massive Star in the Universe? by Phil Plait (March 20, 2026); 5.1 The Scale of Space Will Break Your Brain by Phil Plait (March 8, 2024); 5.2 How Heavy is the Universe? Conflicting Answers Hint at New Physics by Anil Ananthaswamy (May 12, 2020); 5.3 How Many Holes Does the Universe Have? by Manon Bischoff (May 31, 2024); 5.4 Faster-Than-Light Galaxies Are a Fact of Life in Our Expanding Universe by Phil Plait (October 3, 2025); 5.5 What's the Most Distant Galaxy? And Why Does It Matter? by Phil Plait (December 26, 2025); 5.6 JWST Spots Most Distant Galaxy Ever, Pushing the Limits of the Observable Universe by Jackie Flynn Mogensen (January 28, 2026); 5.7 When a Galaxy Erupts, What We See Depends on How We See It by Phil Plait (October 17, 2025); 5.8 Our Milky Way's Warped Disk Keeps Getting Weirder by Phil Plait (November 7, 2025); 5.9 JWST Unveils Most Intricate Map Yet of Cosmic Dark Matter by Joseph Howlett (January 26, 2026); 5.10 JWST's Puzzling Early Galaxies Bend Astrophysics by Jonathan O'Callaghan (February 9, 2024); 5.11 JWST's First Glimpses of Early Galaxies Could Break Cosmology by Jonathan O'Callaghan (September 14, 2022); 5.12 Astronomers Grapple with JWST's Discovery of Early Galaxies by Jonathan O'Callaghan (December 6, 2022); 5.13 JWST's Newfound Galaxies Are the Oldest Ever Seen by Jonathan O'Callaghan (April 13, 2023); 5.14 How Can Galaxies Ever Collide in an Ever-Expanding Universe? by Phil Plait (February 6, 2026); 5.15 Astronomers Witness the Birth of a New Solar System by Joseph Howlett (March 24, 2026).

INDEX